HARRY S. TRUMAN

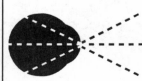

This Large Print Book carries the
Seal of Approval of N.A.V.H.

THE AMERICAN PRESIDENTS

HARRY S. TRUMAN

ROBERT DALLEK
ARTHUR M. SCHLESINGER, JR.

THORNDIKE PRESS
A part of Gale, Cengage Learning

∴ GALE
CENGAGE Learning

Detroit • New York • San Francisco • New Haven, Conn • Waterville, Maine • London

GALE
CENGAGE Learning™

LIBRARY OF CONGRESS CATALOGING-IN-PUBLICATION DATA

Dallek, Robert.
    Harry S. Truman / by Robert Dallek ; Arthur M. Schlesinger,
Jr. and Sean Wilentz, general editors.
      p. cm. — (The American presidents)
    Includes bibliographical references.
    ISBN-13: 978-1-4104-1118-1 (lg. print : hardcover : alk. paper)
    ISBN-10: 1-4104-1118-4 (lg. print : hardcover : alk. paper)
    1. Truman, Harry S., 1884–1972. 2. Presidents—United
States—Biography. 3. United States—Politics and
government—1945–1953. 4. Large type books. I. Schlesinger,
Arthur M. (Arthur Meier), 1917–2007. II. Wilentz, Sean. III.
Title.
    E814.D25 2008b
    973.918092—dc22
    [B]
                                           2008035345

Published in 2008 by arrangement with Henry Holt and Company, LLC.

Printed in the United States of America
1 2 3 4 5 6 7 12 11 10 09 08

For Peter Kovler,
whose support of historical memory
and medical research
has touched so many lives.

CONTENTS

EDITOR'S NOTE

THE AMERICAN PRESIDENCY

The president is the central player in the American political order. That would seem to contradict the intentions of the Founding Fathers. Remembering the horrid example of the British monarchy, they invented a separation of powers in order, as Justice Brandeis later put it, "to preclude the exercise of arbitrary power." Accordingly, they divided the government into three allegedly equal and coordinate branches — the executive, the legislative, and the judiciary.

But a system based on the tripartite separation of powers has an inherent tendency toward inertia and stalemate. One of the three branches must take the initiative if the system is to move. The executive branch alone is structurally capable of taking that initiative. The Founders must have sensed this when they accepted Alexander Hamil-

9

ton's proposition in the Seventieth Federalist that "energy in the executive is a leading character in the definition of good government." They thus envisaged a strong president — but within an equally strong system of constitutional accountability. (The term *imperial presidency* arose in the 1970s to describe the situation when the balance between power and accountability is upset in favor of the executive.)

The American system of self-government thus comes to focus in the presidency — "the vital place of action in the system," as Woodrow Wilson put it. Henry Adams, himself the great-grandson and grandson of presidents as well as the most brilliant of American historians, said that the American president "resembles the commander of a ship at sea. He must have a helm to grasp, a course to steer, a port to seek." The men in the White House (thus far only men, alas) in steering their chosen courses have shaped our destiny as a nation.

Biography offers an easy education in American history, rendering the past more human, more vivid, more intimate, more accessible, more connected to ourselves. Biography reminds us that presidents are not supermen. They are human beings too, worrying about decisions, attending to wives and children, juggling balls in the air, and putting on their pants one leg at a time. Indeed, as Emerson contended, "There is properly no history; only biography."

Presidents serve us as inspirations, and they also serve us as warnings. They provide bad examples as well as good. The nation, the Supreme Court has said, has "no right to expect that it will always have wise and humane rulers, sincerely attached to the principles of the Constitution. Wicked men, ambitious of power, with hatred of liberty and contempt of law, may fill the place once occupied by Washington and Lincoln."

The men in the White House express the ideals and the values, the frailties and the flaws, of the voters who send them there. It is altogether natural that we should want to know more about the virtues and the vices of the fellows we have elected to govern us. As we know more about them, we will know more about ourselves. The French political philosopher Joseph de Maistre said, "Every nation has the government it deserves."

At the start of the twenty-first century, forty-two men have made it to the Oval Office. (George W. Bush is counted our forty-third president, because Grover Cleveland, who served nonconsecutive terms, is counted twice.) Of the parade of presidents, a dozen or so lead the polls periodically conducted by historians and political scientists. What makes a great president?

Great presidents possess, or are possessed by, a vision of an ideal America. Their passion, as they grasp the helm, is to set the ship of state on the right course toward the port they seek. Great presidents also have a deep psychic connection with the needs, anxieties, dreams of people. "I do not believe," said Wilson, "that any man can lead who does not act . . . under the impulse of a profound sympathy with those whom he leads — a sympathy which is insight — an insight which is of the heart rather than of the intellect."

"All of our great presidents," said Franklin D. Roosevelt, "were leaders of thought at a time when certain ideas in the life of the nation had to be clarified." So Washington incarnated the idea of federal union, Jefferson and Jackson the idea of democracy, Lincoln union and freedom, Cleveland rugged honesty. Theodore Roosevelt and Wilson, said FDR, were both "moral leaders, each in his own way and his own time, who used the presidency as a pulpit."

To succeed, presidents not only must have a port to seek but they must convince Congress and the electorate that it is a port worth seeking. Politics in a democracy is ultimately an educational process, an adventure in persuasion and consent. Every president stands in Theodore Roosevelt's bully pulpit.

The greatest presidents in the scholars' rankings, Washington, Lincoln, and Franklin Roosevelt, were leaders who confronted and overcame the republic's greatest crises. Crisis widens presidential opportunities for bold and imaginative action. But it does not guarantee presidential greatness. The crisis of secession did not spur Buchanan or the crisis of depression spur Hoover to creative leadership. Their inadequacies in the face of crisis allowed Lincoln and the second Roosevelt to show the difference individuals make to history. Still, even in the absence of first-order crisis, forceful and persuasive presidents — Jefferson, Jackson, James K. Polk, Theodore Roosevelt, Harry Truman, John F. Kennedy, Ronald Reagan, George W. Bush — are able to impose their own priorities on the country.

The diverse drama of the presidency offers a fascinating set of tales. Biographies of American presidents constitute a chronicle of wisdom and folly, nobility and pettiness, courage and cunning, forthrightness and deceit, quarrel and consensus. The turmoil perennially swirling around the White House illuminates the heart of the American democracy.

It is the aim of the American Presidents series to present the grand panorama of our chief executives in volumes compact enough for the busy reader, lucid enough for the student, authoritative enough for the scholar. Each volume offers a distillation of character and career. I hope that these lives will give readers some understanding of the pitfalls and potentialities of the presidency and also of the responsibilities of citizenship. Truman's famous sign — "The buck stops here" — tells only half the story. Citizens cannot escape the ultimate responsibility. It is in the voting booth, not on the presidential desk, that the buck finally stops.

— Arthur M. Schlesinger, Jr.

1
P RELUDES

Of the eighteen twentieth-century American presidents, beginning with William McKinley and ending with Bill Clinton, only four currently have claims on great or near-great leadership: Theodore Roosevelt, Woodrow Wilson, Franklin Roosevelt, and Harry Truman. Perhaps in time Ronald Reagan and Bill Clinton may join this elite group, but at this juncture such a judgment is premature.

On the face of things, Truman's high standing is surprising. Unlike the two Roosevelts and Wilson — whom nobody would describe by background and education as common men — Truman was notable for his ordinariness. How he rose above the commonplace to become so extraordinary makes Truman's life and career a compelling puzzle. This is not to suggest that either of the Roosevelts or Wilson had easy, uninterrupted trajectories toward greatness. All

15

three had their disappointments and public stumbles. But Truman's erratic course toward distinction was more pronounced, with deeper valleys and less spectacular peaks, except for his stunning upset election victory in 1948.

Truman was entirely mindful of how much his advance toward greatness rested on circumstances beyond his control. "We can never tell what is in store for us," he declared. It was his way of saying that chance had a major — maybe the largest — role in shaping his fortunes, for good and ill. "Most men don't aspire to the presidency," he said after leaving the White House. "It comes to them by accident."[1]

Yet however much he saw uncontrollable circumstances shaping the lives of great men, he never accepted that external events alone would dictate his fate. Like so many of his predecessors in the White House, Harry Truman was a driven man. "An insatiable demand for recognition," one of his biographers observes, was a dominant feature of his rise to prominence.[2] He was confident that personal ambition could make a difference in every life. Like Shakespeare's Julius Caesar, who saw "a tide in the affairs of men, which taken at the flood, leads on to fortune," Truman took "the current when it serve[d]." He shared a conviction with millions of other Americans that self-fulfillment was a noble calling, the Horatio Alger belief in success through good character and hard work bolstered by good fortune. As the novelist Thomas Wolfe put it, "To every man his chance — to every man, regardless of his birth . . . to become whatever thing his manhood and his vision can combine to make him — this seeker, is the promise of America."[3] Truman's biography gives credence to Wolfe's conviction.

Harry Truman's path to the country's highest elected office was never linear. Enough setbacks marked his prepresidential career to have tested the character of the most resilient of men, and perhaps encourage a belief in miracles.

Born on May 8, 1884, Truman spent his first six years on southern Missouri farms, where he had memories of a comfortable and even "wonderful" life typical of many other nineteenth-century, largely self-sufficient farm families. In 1890, the Trumans moved to Independence, a town of six thousand people ten miles southeast of Kansas City. Although it was a rough frontier center with no public utilities or paved streets, Independence had public schools at which Harry and a younger brother and sister could receive schooling unavailable in their more isolated farm community.[4]

When Harry graduated from high school in 1901, he wanted to attend the United States Military Academy, but poor eyesight, which required him to wear glasses with thick lenses, barred him from West Point. That year, when Harry's father, John Truman, a commodity-livestock trader and speculator, began suffering a series of losses that bankrupted the family, Truman's possible interest in higher education fell victim to his family's economic needs. He went to work for the Santa Fe Railroad as a payroll clerk and then as a bank clerk in Kansas City until 1906, when his father, who had resumed farming, pressed his son into giving up his ample $100-a-month job to join him in running the family farm. For the next eleven years, Truman worked long days, through good times and bad, planting and harvesting crops, raising and selling livestock.

During this time, he also maintained a long-standing interest in reading biography and military and political history. "I saw that it takes men to make history or that there would be no history," he wrote in his postpresidential *Memoirs*.[5] He gave expression to his fascination with the military by joining a local National Guard artillery unit in 1905, serving in its summer encampments and attending its drill sessions on and off until 1911. After two tours of duty, however, the demands of the farm decided him against a third three-year enlistment.

In 1917, when the United States entered World War I, Truman reenlisted in his National Guard battery unit. It was entirely voluntary; at thirty-three, he was past draft age. But President Wilson's call to arms appealed to his belief in a larger good: "I felt that I was a Galahad after the Grail," he wrote in an autobiography.[6] But more than patriotic idealism motivated him; he could have just as easily served the cause by staying on the farm to help supply food to America's allies. More to the point, Truman had hopes of using military service as a launching pad for a political career. The competition for office and chance to gain distinction through public service fascinated him. "If I were real rich," he wrote in a letter to Elizabeth (Bess) Wallace, his future wife, "I'd just as soon spend my money buying votes and offices as yachts and autos." And yet he was under no illusions; as he told Bess in the same letter, "To succeed politically, [a man] must be an egoist or a fool or a ward boss tool."[7]

His father had introduced him to local and national politics as a teenager. In 1900, when he was sixteen, they attended the Democratic National Convention in Kansas City, where the party made William Jennings Bryan its presidential nominee for the second time.[8] Truman remembered running errands for a local leader during the convention, which took place in a "great hall" holding seventeen thousand delegates and onlookers, who responded to Bryan's nominating speech with a boisterous half-hour demonstration. In subsequent years, Truman involved himself in local Democratic Party politics, winning appointments as a town postmaster and as a road overseer, responsible for the maintenance of county highways. By 1917, he understood that wartime military service could be of benefit not only to the country but also to someone with aspirations for elected office.

Despite having been out of his Guard unit for six years, Truman still had close ties to many of his fellow soldiers. These friendships, combined with a genial temperament that greatly appealed to most everyone who knew him, led to his election as a first lieutenant. (The Missouri state guard, reflecting a long-standing antagonism to a military dominated by professional soldiers, chose its own officers.) "Because of my efforts to get along with my associates," Truman recalled, "I was usually able to get what I wanted."[9] During training exercises near Fort Sill, Oklahoma, he demonstrated keen leadership abilities that soon won him a promotion to captain.

In France, he acquitted himself beyond his highest hopes. After being given command of the least disciplined battery in his regiment — one that had already blighted the careers of two officers — Truman quickly won the respect of his men with a combination of toughness and fairness. At the same time, despite the challenge of mastering the French 75-millimeter cannon, which required math and engineering classes well above anything he had studied in high school, he developed the necessary skills to become an effective artillery officer. At the end of seven weeks in combat, his battery had suffered only one dead and one wounded, and he received a commendation from his division's commanding general for his battlefield performance.[10]

In May 1919, after he was mustered out of the army, his highest priorities were to marry Bess Wallace, which he did in June, and give up farming for a business enterprise that could provide a comfortable living as a prelude to winning an elected office. Within days of leaving the army, he and Eddie Jacobson, an army buddy also from Kansas City, laid plans to open a haberdashery shop in a choice downtown locale. Unfortunately, a postwar recession beginning in 1920 doomed their venture and left them with considerable debts.[11]

But Truman was not dissuaded from running for county office. He saw the path to a successful election through establishing the widest possible contacts and tying himself to Kansas City's power brokers, the political machine run by Tom Pendergast and his family.[12] Like President Warren G. Harding, who had begun his career in Ohio politics as a "joiner" of numerous fraternal organizations, Truman became an active member of several civic, service, and veterans' associations, including the American Legion and the Veterans of Foreign Wars. He saw his participation in these groups as essential for business success and as a means to win support from influential leaders for his candidacy.[13]

In 1922, as a veteran with ties to influential business and social leaders in Kansas City and Independence, Truman impressed the Pendergasts as someone who could win the eastern district judgeship of Jackson County. Along with a western district judge and a presiding judge or chairman, the three officials administered the county's affairs. The judgeships were irresistible prizes for a political machine: they controlled numerous patronage jobs as well as the power to assign contracts, particularly for the repair and maintenance of county roads. Truman won his first election by 279 votes out of nearly 12,000 cast for him and three opponents.

Truman's two-year term was a rude introduction to the uncertainties of a political life.[14] Although he and his fellow judges managed nearly to halve the county's debt of $1.2 million and won praise from the local press for having improved the quality of the county's roads by rigorous insistence on proper maintenance, Truman nonetheless lost his reelection bid in 1924. Despite a successful primary campaign, which he won by sixteen hundred votes — over 56 percent of the total count — he could not withstand a national and local Republican onslaught in November. With Calvin Coolidge winning handily over John W. Davis at the national level and some Jackson County Democrats, alienated by Pendergast's refusal to give them a fuller share of county spoils, abandoning their party, Truman lost to his Republican opponent by a five-point margin, 52.5 percent to 47.5 percent.[15]

But he would spend only a short time in the political wilderness. During the two years before he could run again, he sold memberships in the Kansas City Automobile Club, emphasizing his knowledge of road hazards as reasons for folks to insure themselves against highway breakdowns. While making enough of a living from his effectiveness as a salesman, his investments in two failed bank enterprises convinced him that however uncertain running for political office might be, it was a more reliable career for a middle-aged man with no record of consistent success at anything, except for his two-year army service.

With the Pendergasts outmaneuvering their Democratic Party opponents in 1925 to ensure that they would be "the boss of bosses in Kansas City politics" for the foreseeable future, Truman's ties to the machine ensured his return to office in 1926. This time he ran for presiding judge, and he won a convincing victory in the November general election, with 56 percent of the vote.[16]

Harry Truman's eight years as presiding judge of Jackson County was an exercise in compromised ethics, in the service of his personal ambition and the larger good. Truman turned a blind eye to the voracious appetite of the Pendergast machine for public offices that netted its bosses financial returns equal to the earnings of the area's most successful businessmen. "I wonder if I did the right thing to put a lot of no account sons of bitches on the payroll and pay other sons of bitches more money for supplies than they were worth in order to satisfy the political powers and save [the county] $3,500,000," he confided to a private record he made of his tenure.[17]

Although he had numerous second thoughts about staying on the job and suffered hidden emotional strains over having to deal with the corruption that was a fixture of Kansas City politics, he rationalized his continuing presence as presiding judge by devoting himself to the effective deliverance of public services: good roads, well-regarded public schools, a county hospital providing up-to-date medical care, humane treatment of indigents, and proper law enforcement by the police and the courts — all provided without budgetary overruns requiring higher taxes. He took satisfaction in maintaining his own integrity, never skimming money from the many contracts he negotiated, and the pleasure of helping people who could not help themselves. This was especially the case with the onset of the Great Depression in 1930, when city and county unemployment reached historic heights and the jobless relied on local government for make-work and charity to feed and clothe them. He thought of himself as a practical idealist, who was making the best of an imperfect world.

After two terms as presiding judge, however, it was accepted practice for him to move on. He wanted to run for governor of Missouri, especially after the machine's candidate died suddenly in October 1932, just a month before the election. But Tom Pendergast, the machine's boss, vetoed the suggestion, telling Harry that in two years he could run for Congress or the county collector's job, which paid $10,000 a year.

It was another low moment in Truman's political career. He advised a nephew to shun politics for banking or some other commercial enterprise, cynically declaring that an elected office taught you nothing and left the incumbent vulnerable to changing political circumstances. When Harry asked Tom Pendergast in early 1934 to fulfill his promise and support him in a congressional campaign, Pendergast explained that someone else had already been selected for the seat. By April, as Truman approached the age of fifty, the only thing he thought he could look forward to was "a virtual pension in some minor county office."[18]

But in May 1934 came an extraordinary and unpredictable turn of fate. With Franklin Roosevelt and the New Deal riding a popular political wave, the Democrats' chances of defeating the incumbent Republican U.S. senator Roscoe C. Patterson seemed better than good. A leading contender for the nomination was Jacob (Tuck) Milligan, a six-term congressman and an ally of Senator Bennett C. Clark, Tom Pendergast's rival for control of Missouri party politics. Pendergast gave substantial thought to who should carry his banner in this crucial statewide contest, which could have large consequences for his machine. Pendergast approached four party stalwarts to run — retired U.S. senator Jim Reed, Congressman Joe Shannon, Kansas City attorney Charles Howell (who had lost a Democratic primary bid for a Senate seat to Clark in 1932), and Jim Aylward, the Democratic Party state chairman. None of them wanted to do it.

That left Harry Truman; his eight successful years as Jackson County's presiding judge and his substantial contacts in both the rural and urban areas of the state made him a reasonable alternative. Although Truman doubted that he could find the money for an effective campaign and suggested that he wait to run for governor in 1936, Pendergast refused to take no for an answer. He needed Truman to run, and he would supply the money. Truman's objections concealed a sense of exhilaration at having "come to the place where all men strive to be at my age."[19]

The three-month campaign leading up to the primary vote on August 7 pitted Truman against not only Milligan but also Congressman Jack Cochran from St. Louis, who represented the interests of that city's political machine. The smart money was betting on Cochran, but Milligan's competition for St. Louis and rural votes reduced the odds in Cochran's favor.

The three candidates tried to outdo one another in identifying themselves with a popular president and with New Deal programs that sought to provide economic relief and hope for a swift end to the Depression. Since neither Milligan nor Cochran could best Truman in their claims to be Roosevelt's strongest supporter, they attacked him for his ties to Pendergast and for being his stooge. But whatever doubts they raised about him with voters, it was Truman's affiliation with the machine and its statewide support from men and women who had been the beneficiaries of the organization's largesse that served his campaign best. His own contacts with officials in Missouri's 113 other counties, built up over his eight years of service as Jackson County presiding judge, was a decisive element in helping him win votes across the state.

It was a nasty campaign that descended into ugly name-calling. Senator Clark attacked Truman for his "mendacity and imbecility," while Truman accused Milligan of putting relatives on his congressional payroll and charged Clark with having won his Senate seat by trading on the reputation of his father, Champ Clark, the former Speaker of the House of Representatives. Bennett Clark's performance in office, Truman declared, demonstrated that there was not much to be said for inherited talent. Tom Pendergast weighed in with press leaks about Bennett Clark paying him a visit at his office in Kansas City to discuss politics, suggesting that Clark was not above seeking an arrangement with his machine.[20]

The final tally on August 7 gave Truman a 40,000-vote plurality over Cochran and 129,000 more votes than Milligan, who ran third. Of Truman's 276,850 votes, 137,529, almost half of his total, came from Jackson County, where Cochran received only 1,525 votes. Similarly, Truman won the backing of only 4,614 St. Louis voters.

Riding the Roosevelt wave in the November election, Truman bested Senator Patterson by more than 250,000 votes out of 1.3 million cast. Even so, Truman saw his primary and general election victories as little more than good timing that might not replicate themselves six years later. "It'll be safer to rent than to buy, of course," he told a reporter about his search for living quarters in Washington, D.C.[21] However pleased he was at becoming one of ninety-six senators in a country of 130 million people, he had not lost sight of how uncertain the career of any elected official could be and the challenges he faced in the nation's capital. "I was timid as a country boy arriving on the campus of a great university for his first year," he recalled in his *Memoirs*.[22] The *New York Times* was less charitable; it described the new senator from Missouri as "a rube from Pendergast land."[23]

At the outset, Truman struggled with self-doubt about his worthiness for the office. But advice from the veteran senator J. Hamilton Lewis of Illinois helped ease his concern: "Harry, don't start out with an inferiority complex," Lewis told him. "For the first six months you'll wonder how the hell you got here, and after that you'll wonder how the hell the rest of us got here."[24] In time, Truman saw the truth of Lewis's point. Though there were some senators he held in high regard, he came to feel that he was no less qualified to hold his seat than most of his colleagues.

Nevertheless, neither circumstances nor his performance in office marked him out as a distinguished senator during his first years on Capitol Hill.[25] When Truman arrived in January 1935, the Democrats held sixty-nine of the ninety-six Senate seats, a majority that grew to seventy-one to twenty-five after Roosevelt's landslide reelection in 1936. Such large majorities diminished Truman's importance to the White House, which saw little need to court a freshman senator who seemed likely to vote with the president without much stroking or prodding. And in fact Truman needed few inducements to follow the president's lead, so sympathetic was he to Roosevelt's legislative initiatives.

By contrast, Bennett Clark, who was a less certain supporter, received far more White House attention and backing for patronage requests than Truman. A Kansas City journalist described Truman sitting "in the back row of the top-heavy Democratic side of the Senate at every session, listening, absorbing, learning. . . . His is the conventional way. He ruffles no oldsters' feathers, treads on no toes."[26] He followed House Speaker Sam Rayburn's famous advice to all newcomers — to get along, go along.

Truman's appointment to the Interstate Commerce Committee gave him the opportunity to chair a subcommittee investigating railroads, which struggled during the Depression against financial collapse. Popular antagonism to big business in the thirties fueled Truman's committee hearings, which concluded that exploitative Wall Street bankers and lawyers were fostering the railroad's problems. Truman led efforts to pass regulatory legislation that would make the railroads less vulnerable to "wasteful and destructive competition." But conflicts between labor and business interests blocked passage of a bill that Truman had made the major legislative effort of his term.[27]

Normally, a one-term senator of a majority party running on the same ticket with a popular president would be the odds-on favorite for reelection. But this was not the case for Harry Truman in 1940. After six years in the Senate, he had no significant legislative initiative to his credit, and his close identity with Tom Pendergast in 1940 was now a major liability.

In 1939, Pendergast had been convicted of tax evasion and sent to prison for fifteen months. Although the IRS and Justice Department, with overt White House support, had brought Pendergast down, Truman refused to abandon his ally, who had done so much to facilitate his political career. To the contrary, he stubbornly defended Pendergast, publicly attacking his prosecution as a witch hunt by Republican judges out to undermine Jackson County's Democratic organization. With the Roosevelt administration so actively involved in Pendergast's demise, however, it made Truman look like an uncritical partisan turning a blind eye to his mentor's corruption. He considered not running again in 1940, but when he decided to do it anyway, he told Bess, "The terrible things done by the high ups in K.C. will be a lead weight on me from now on."[28]

With FDR offering no support and the

Missouri press opposing him, Truman understood that, despite his incumbency, he was the underdog in the primary against a popular Missouri governor, Lloyd Stark. Truman was "a dead cock in the pit," declared Missouri's leading newspaper, the *St. Louis Post Dispatch*.[29] But Truman pulled off a minor miracle. His outspoken backing of the New Deal, his strong support of military preparedness in a time of international danger, and Stark's failings as a candidate — his self-importance and simultaneous attempt to win the vice presidential nomination — gave Truman an 8,000-vote margin out of 665,000 ballots cast. In November, Missouri gave Roosevelt its electoral support for a third time and returned Truman to the Senate, though this time with only 51 percent of the statewide vote.[30]

As had been the case so often in Truman's life, fate or circumstances intervened after 1940 to change his fortunes. American involvement in the war lifted him to a prominence no one could have anticipated. Even before the Pearl Harbor attack in December 1941 that brought America into the fighting, Truman had found a public cause that set him apart from his Senate colleagues. With industrial mobilization spurred by Roosevelt's announced determination in December 1940 to make America "the arsenal of democracy," Truman seized on allegations of waste and fraud by defense contractors to begin an investigation. He was now the chairman of a Military Affairs subcommittee, and in that role he sought to reduce profiteering and make the national arms buildup less costly and more effective.

In January 1941, after traveling to a number of military facilities and defense plants in the South and the Midwest, where he personally saw waste and profiteering that cried out for correction, he proposed to lead a formal investigation. Although the White House was not keen on a congressional probe that might slow down its preparedness efforts, Roosevelt signed on to Truman's proposal as a way to head off an investigation by a less friendly House committee.

Nearly every member of Truman's seven-member committee — five Democrats and two Republicans — was a relatively unknown senator. (The exception was Tom Connally, a popular senator from Texas.) Their hearings helped to change this. In the spring of 1941, they visited army bases, where they made news by describing the excess costs of industrial mobilization and the need for ongoing scrutiny to improve the process. By the fall, the committee's success in unearthing waste and winning headlines produced a larger budget and the addition of three more senators, one Democrat and two Republicans, who saw committee membership as both a national service and a political advantage.

The Truman Committee's evenhanded criticism of the military, industry, labor, and the administration's Office of Production Management (OPM) gave it compelling influence with the Congress, the White House, the press, and the public. It forced the president to replace a sprawling OPM with a War Production Board under a single director who could streamline the allocation of raw materials, the granting of contracts, and the buildup of armaments that could supply the war machines of America and its allies.

Between 1942 and 1944, the Truman Committee held hundreds of hearings and issued dozens of reports that won almost unanimous praise from the press and the public for saving billions of dollars and advancing the war effort. *Time* put Harry Truman's picture on the cover of the magazine and called his committee's work America's "first line of defense." A poll of journalists about the ten most important contributors to the war effort in Washington included Truman, the only member of Congress to win such an accolade. Others described the committee's work as "the most successful congressional investigative effort in American history." If, according to Truman's biographer Alonzo Hamby, the committee's work wasn't quite as productive or important as many at the time thought, its success came from its ability to reflect patriotic national sentiment about winning the war and putting checks on big business, labor unions, and government bureaucracies.[31]

In 1944, as the presidential election campaign began and rumors abounded about whether Roosevelt would retain Vice President Henry Wallace, Harry Truman's meteoric rise put his name on everybody's short list for the second spot on the ticket. It wasn't simply luck that had brought Truman to this moment, however. His determination to chair an investigative committee on national defense rested on an eagerness not only to serve the country but also to put himself on a par with earlier Senate giants who commanded an enduring place in the country's history. That he was now projected into the mix of vice presidential possibilities was nothing he foresaw, but he welcomed the attention as a demonstration that he had established himself as much more than the senator from Pendergast.

Truman's nomination for the vice presidency in 1944 is one of those political events shrouded in mystery that will never be entirely unraveled. "The President never . . . pursued a more Byzantine course than in his handling of this question," Roosevelt's biographer James MacGregor Burns says.[32]

By the beginning of that year, it was clear that Vice President Wallace was a divisive force in the Democratic Party. His identification with ultraliberals who favored expanding the New Deal at the first opportunity did not sit well with party conservatives, chiefly southerners. They opposed any additional expansion of federal authority at the expense of the states and localities, which they feared could mean an assault on the traditional segregation of the races. And even in the North, many were inclined to inhibit further growth of federal bureaucracies and labor unions after the war was won, making them unsympathetic to retaining Wallace, who would be in line to succeed an unhealthy president, whether or not he survived a fourth term.

Wallace had the additional problem of being a bit strange — a man, the journalist Allen Drury said, who "looks like a hayseed, talks like a prophet, and acts like an embarrassed schoolboy."[33] Or, as Truman's biographer David McCullough put it, "Wallace was too intellectual, a mystic who spoke Russian. . . . He was too remote, too controversial, too liberal — much too liberal, which was the main charge against him."[34]

Roosevelt, who refused to give an unequivocal endorsement to any candidate, which could alienate one or another faction within the party, encouraged several people, including Wallace, to think he would back them for the vice presidency. But Roosevelt demonstrated his intention to dump Wallace by sending him on a fact-finding trip to China and Russia in the spring of 1944. It was meant to prevent Wallace from personally pushing his candidacy in the period immediately before the Democratic convention.

Roosevelt played a similar game with James Byrnes, former South Carolina senator and Supreme Court associate justice, who became the director of the Office of War Mobilization in 1943 and was known as the "assistant president." Byrnes had broad national support for his war work and was favored by the conservative wing of the party. Although Roosevelt dropped hints that he preferred Byrnes as his running mate, he was reluctant to elevate someone who was unsympathetic to a number of New Deal measures. To promote interest in a convention that lacked the drama of a presidential nomination fight and maintain backing for himself among all party factions, Roosevelt indicated possible interest in awarding the prize to Speaker of the House Sam Rayburn, Senator Alben Barkley of Kentucky, Supreme Court Justice William O. Douglas, and Harry Truman, as well as Wallace and Byrnes.

At the end of the day, Roosevelt and the party's bosses saw Truman as the best alternative. He was a solid New Deal supporter from a border state with ties to conservatives and liberals. His reputation for honesty and patriotism were unimpeachable. Alongside of Wallace and Byrnes, he was the perfect staunch but moderate Democrat — "the second Missouri compromise," one wit called him. He was "the mousy little man from Missouri," *Time* derisively said.[35] But did it matter all that much? Truman would be serving in the shadow of a larger-than-life president who, at the end of a fourth term, could anoint anyone he wanted to succeed him. After four years, Harry Truman would likely join the ranks of those many other vice presidents who fell into obscurity and shared Woodrow Wilson's observation that there is nothing to say about the vice presidency and after you've said that, there's nothing more to say.[36]

Except for a lunch meeting at the White House in August, Truman had no direct contact with the president during the campaign. Truman traveled the length of the country by train and spoke warmly on Roosevelt's behalf. Despite attacks on Truman as unfit for the presidency, implying that Roosevelt might not make it through another term, the outcome of the election had nothing to do with Truman. It was Roosevelt versus his Republican opponent, Governor Thomas E. Dewey of New York. And although the margin of victory was the smallest of his four elections, Roosevelt won by 3.5 million out of 47 million popular votes, and topped Dewey by four to one in the electoral college, 432 to 99.

In apparent agreement with Wilson, Roosevelt saw Truman alone only twice during the eighty-two days he served as vice president. True, the president was in Washington for only thirty days after his fourth inauguration on January 20, 1945, but during that time he gave no indication that he intended to give Truman any special role. Most telling, Roosevelt never discussed the imminent development of an atomic bomb with his new vice president.[37] One journalist, who spent a lot of time with Truman after he became vice president, told another reporter, "Truman doesn't know what's going on. Roosevelt won't tell him anything."[38]

And this, despite Roosevelt's failing health. Severe hypertension and congestive heart failure had made it apparent to some people close to the president that his days were numbered. When Lord Moran, Winston Churchill's physician, saw Roosevelt at the Yalta conference in February 1945, he concluded from his ashen appearance, loss of weight, trembling hands, and slow speech that he was suffering from hardening of the arteries of the brain and would not live for more than another few months.[39] Roosevelt's failure to confide in Truman may have indicated that he believed he could survive his fourth term. He made a point of not asking his doctors about his medical condition, which allowed him to deny his physical decline and the need to prepare Truman for a possible succession.

Although Truman understood that the

president's health might be a problem, he was no more prepared for his sudden death than anyone else. When Truman returned a call from the White House late on the afternoon of April 12, 1945, he was told to come over at once. The urgency in White House secretary Steve Early's voice made Truman uneasy. Though he paled, muttered, "Jesus Christ and General Jackson," and ran through the Capitol to his office and then a waiting car to speed him down Pennsylvania Avenue, he shut out thoughts of disaster by imagining that the president was back in town and simply wanted to discuss some congressional assignment with him.

Ushered up to the president's quarters, Truman found himself in a room with the First Lady, Eleanor Roosevelt. She delivered the news: "Harry, the president is dead."

When he found his voice, a stunned Truman asked, "Is there anything I can do for you?"

Mrs. Roosevelt replied, "Is there anything we can do for you, Harry? For you are the one in trouble now."[40]

Truman said later that he felt as if he had "been struck by a bolt of lightning." He told a group of reporters the next day that it was as if "the moon, the stars and the planets had all fallen on me."[41] And in a sense they had. A vice president with no national executive experience was now to replace the longest-serving and most revered president since Lincoln, in the midst of a world war. Neither Truman nor anyone else could imagine how he would bring the war to a conclusion and measure up to what promised to be daunting postwar challenges at home and abroad.

2
ENDING THE WAR
AND PLANNING THE
PEACE

Truman's shocked response to the death of
Franklin Roosevelt reflected the country's
troubled feelings about what his passing
might mean for the future. Most Americans
could not imagine having an unproven
political leader in the White House with the
world still at war and the aftermath of the
fighting unsettled, and Truman understood
the public's doubts.

But in the days immediately after assum-
ing the presidency, Truman took to heart
his old friend Senator Alben Barkley's
advice. "Have confidence in yourself," Barkley told him. "If you do not, the people
will lose confidence in you."[1]

Truman appreciated that the best way to
reassure the country and build public support for himself was by demonstrating his
determination to fulfill Roosevelt's stated
wartime and postwar plans. After being
sworn in as president on April 12, he

directed Secretary of State Edward Stettinius to announce that the United Nations organizing conference scheduled for April 25 in San Francisco would meet as planned. In a nationally broadcast radio speech before a joint session of Congress on April 16, the day after Roosevelt was buried in Hyde Park, Truman promised to pursue his predecessor's aim of unconditional surrender by the Axis powers.

Events in Europe at the end of April and the beginning of May cooperated with Truman's pronouncement. Italy's Benito Mussolini was assassinated by antifascist partisans, signaling the total collapse of his regime, and Germany's unconditional surrender followed Adolf Hitler's suicide in a Berlin bunker.

Despite being so much in Roosevelt's shadow, Truman took office with a broad base of public support; at the beginning of June, he enjoyed an 87 percent approval rating according to a Gallup poll. His personal qualities were his most attractive feature to the public. "What one thing do you like best about the way Harry Truman is handling his job?" Gallup asked. "His honesty, sincerity, and friendliness," a plurality of respondents said.[2]

Despite the public's affinity for the new

president's common touch, Truman's high ratings rested principally on his association with the prompt and decisive end to the war in Europe. He understood that had the struggle against Germany dragged on and threatened to produce less than unconditional surrender, it would have raised serious questions about his effectiveness as president. Consequently, he worried that if ending the Pacific war came at a heavy cost in American troops and if postwar arrangements in Europe and Japan were less favorable than what Americans expected, his public standing would take a tumble.

His eagerness for a quick and complete Japanese surrender mainly rested on his concern about saving American lives, but he also knew that confidence in his leadership was bound up with a smooth transition to a postwar world. A genuine concern with the long-term national and international well-being muted whatever pride he took from acquitting himself effectively as chief executive.

To sustain public enthusiasm for the war effort and for himself, he believed it essential to project a degree of optimism that did not reflect his private worries about the Soviet Union's promises to enter the war against Japan and the likely American casualties of an invasion of the Japanese home islands. Nearly 400,000 troops had already died in the war, and the fewer additional fatalities, the better.

Though Truman had no experience in making major military decisions or conducting diplomacy, he took comfort from the thought that what he faced now was similar to the earlier challenges he had managed to overcome in his public career. He had relied successfully on his extensive reading of history and biography, especially about political leaders, and on his instincts for what he understood to be politically viable.

Yet he quickly saw that none of the tough political opponents he had encountered in Missouri or in the Senate measured up to the tests posed by the Soviet Union. Part of Moscow's price for joining the Pacific fighting seemed to be Allied acceptance of its control of Eastern Europe, especially Poland. Truman saw this as an unacceptable violation of the commitments that Joseph Stalin made at the Yalta conference to support freely elected governments in the liberated countries. When Truman met with Soviet foreign minister Vyacheslav Molotov at the White House on April 23, he insisted on adherence to postwar democratic arrangements in the nations under Moscow's control. He gave Molotov what he later described as "the one-two, right to the jaw."

Yet Molotov was not overtly intimidated. Neither then nor at the UN organizing conference in San Francisco did Molotov show much inclination to meet American demands. He gave no indication of allowing free elections in Poland or anywhere else Soviet forces had power in Eastern Europe. Moreover, in San Francisco, Molotov insisted on the right of individual UN Security Council members to block discussion of any issues that might interfere with their sovereign rights.

Soviet behavior at the organizing conference provoked a series of newspaper articles describing the erosion, if not the collapse, of Soviet-American cooperation. As British prime minister Winston Churchill told Truman in a May 12 telegram, "An iron curtain is drawn down upon their [the Soviet] front. We do not know what is going on behind."[3]

Determined to avert a break with Russia, Truman decided to send Harry Hopkins, one of Roosevelt's principal advisers and a liaison to Stalin, to Moscow at the end of May. It symbolized Truman's intention to sustain Roosevelt's working relationship with the Soviet leader by trying to find

49

grounds for continued cooperation. When Hopkins, with Truman's acquiescence, all but conceded Soviet control of Poland, Stalin affirmed his determination to enter the war against Japan, abandoned Soviet demands for a veto over Security Council agenda items, and agreed to meet with Truman and Churchill at Potsdam outside of Berlin in July. Out of a hope that Stalin actually intended to maintain good relations with the West and a conviction that the Soviets' entrance into the Pacific war was essential to save thousands of American lives, Truman now publicly declared that Stalin's concessions demonstrated that "the Russians are just as anxious to get along with us as we are with them."[4]

The Potsdam conference, which began on July 17 and lasted until August 2, tested Truman's hopes. During the conference, Winston Churchill's Conservative Party was defeated in the British parliamentary election, and he was replaced as prime minister by the Labour Party leader Clement Attlee. This turn of events made it more difficult to pressure Stalin into concessions. As new heads of their governments, who might prove to be less cooperative than their predecessors, neither Truman nor Attlee could hope to have the sort of influence over

Stalin that Roosevelt and Churchill might have exerted. Truman and Attlee could not possibly command the grudging respect Stalin might at least have shown the men with whom he had collaborated in destroying Hitler and the Nazis.

Truman's interactions with Stalin and his Soviet colleagues during the two and a half weeks in Potsdam deepened his suspicions and doubts about his ability to get along with them. True, he came away from the talks with a reaffirmation of the Soviet promise to fight Japan, his principal reason for the meeting, but Soviet inflexibility about Poland, Eastern Europe generally, and Germany left him frustrated and skeptical of the prospects for future cooperation. He disliked the Soviets' stubborn refusal to compromise on British and American demands, especially Truman's proposal for freedom of navigation on major European waterways. Where Truman saw this as likely to diminish chances of future international conflicts, Stalin saw it as a stealth design for spying on the Soviet Union.

Privately, Truman denounced the Soviets as running a "police government pure and simple. A few top hands just take clubs, pistols and concentration camps and rule people on the lower levels," he confided to

51

a diary.[5] Yet at the same time, he was not without regard for Stalin, whom he said he liked. Given Soviet suffering at the hands of the Germans (more than twenty million Soviet citizens were believed to have perished in the war), Truman found understandable, if not entirely acceptable, Stalin's tough defense of his country's interests.

Publicly, Truman gave Americans a positive report about the meetings, acknowledging that the conversations produced compromises rather than harmonious agreement on all conference items.[6] But he kept his doubts about Stalin and Soviet intentions largely to himself. His true concerns, however, registered in an exchange with Stalin about America's development of the atomic bomb.

The bomb was one of the best-kept secrets of World War II, at least in the United States. Despite a Roosevelt-Churchill agreement signed in 1944 to exclude Moscow from sharing in the control and use of atomic power, Soviet agents had informed the Kremlin of U.S. and British work on the bomb. Truman, who had indirect indications of the effort to build "a secret weapon that will be a wonder" before taking office, did not learn about the Manhattan Project, as it was called, until after Roosevelt's death, when he was briefed by Secretary of War Henry Stimson. (He did not receive substantial detail on the project until April 25, thirteen days after taking office.) And although there is no direct evidence that Truman was told about the 1944 Roosevelt-Churchill agreement, it was clear to him that the Soviets had not been informed of the joint Anglo-American effort to build a bomb.

Because no one knew if the bomb would work until it was tested, Truman made no move to tell Stalin. At the end of May, an interim committee Truman appointed to discuss the use of the bomb decided against inviting Soviet representatives to view the initial weapon's test. Although the committee wished to ensure "every effort to better our political relations with Russia," it also wished "to make certain that we stay ahead" of them.[7]

On July 16 and 18, while he was at Potsdam, Truman received initial reports of the bomb's successful test at Alamogordo in the New Mexico desert. It wasn't until July 21, however, that he received a full account of the weapon's devastating power, a report that "immensely pleased" him, Stimson recorded. "The President was tremendously pepped up by it and spoke to me again and again when I saw him. He said it gave him an entirely new feeling of confidence." Churchill noted that Truman was "markedly more assertive and considerably firmer in rejecting Soviet demands" that day.[8]

Still, Truman was in no hurry to share the news with Stalin; he waited three days, until July 24, to say anything. At the conclusion of an afternoon meeting, Truman recalled, he "casually mentioned to Stalin that we had a new weapon of unusual destructive force. The Russian Premier showed no special interest. All he said was that he was glad to hear it and hoped we would make 'good use of it against the Japanese.' "[9] By being so casual about revealing the news, Truman tried to blunt any suspicion Stalin might harbor that the Americans were trying to intimidate him, which was exactly the response Truman hoped to achieve. But prior knowledge of the Manhattan Project had forearmed Stalin and allowed him to show studied indifference.

Stalin's impassive reaction may have added to Truman's decision the next day to confirm an order to go forward with plans to use the bomb against Japan. Intimidating the Soviets, however, was a relatively minor part of Truman's decision to proceed with an attack. He was much more focused on forcing Japan into a prompt acceptance of unconditional surrender, though one consideration was the possibility of ending the Pacific war before the Soviets even entered the fighting against Japan. Again, this was never the principal reason for using the bomb to speed Japan's defeat; it was a relatively minor part of the equation.

For more than half a century, an argument has raged over whether Truman needed to use the atomic bomb to end the war. Those who have answered in the negative assert that Japan was on its last legs and that a blockade of the home islands, possibly coupled with a demonstration of the bomb's power, could have precipitated a collapse. Truman's impatience, they assert, not only caused the horrific deaths of tens of thousands of Japanese but also left the United States with the moral burden of having been the only nation in history to have used an atomic bomb. After all, they add, it wasn't as if Truman was unmindful of the historical implications of using such a weapon. General Dwight Eisenhower hoped the United States would not have to use so "forcible and destructive" a weapon.[10] Henry Stimson had made clear his fear that atomic power might lead to the complete destruction of civilization. Truman himself saw it as "the most terrible bomb in the history of the world." He thought its development might be the fulfillment of the biblical warning of "the fire destruction prophesied in the Euphrates Valley Era after Noah and the fabulous Ark."[11]

Truman's critics also observe that the Big Three missed an opportunity at Potsdam to induce Japan's prompt surrender. The Japanese had signaled an interest in having the Soviets act as intermediaries in peace talks and might have been ready to end the fighting if the United States had indicated a willingness to maintain the emperor on the throne. But because the United States would not settle for anything less than unconditional surrender, the Potsdam Declaration demanded it without qualification, saying nothing about the emperor's fate or his continuing presence as the symbolic leader of the nation. Critics believe that because Truman did agree in the end to keep the emperor, it was a serious error to have foreclosed this avenue. Instead, the declaration warned of the total defeat of Japan's armed forces and the "utter devastation of the Japanese homeland" unless Tokyo agreed to end the war at once.[12]

Truman and the subsequent defenders of his decision saw plenty of justification for using the atomic bomb, arguing that Tokyo had shown no serious interest in accepting unconditional surrender as the price of peace. From everything Truman and his advisers saw, the Japanese were intent on forcing the Americans to invade their home islands, where they hoped to make them pay a terrible price in casualties. Intercepted cables from Tokyo to its ambassador in Moscow, who had been urging consideration of unconditional surrender, indicated that Japan's government had no interest in making peace on these terms. Japan's rejection of Truman's public demands in May and July for surrender underscored the conviction in Washington that the country would give up only after an invasion or in response to devastating atom bomb attacks.

Nothing weighed on Truman more heavily than the losses that American troops would suffer in an invasion of Japan's home islands. The U.S. casualties in the island-hopping campaign, most recently in Okinawa, were seen as a prelude for what would happen in an offensive against the homeland. In these battles, Japanese troops had refused to give up despite the certainty of defeat, and if this experience was any indication of what was to come, the U.S. military chiefs anticipated between 250,000 and 500,000 American deaths in an invasion, which would be roughly equal to all U.S. troop losses to that point in the war. "I could not bear this thought," Truman said, "and it led to the decision to use the atomic bomb." He had come to "the awful conclusion that it would probably be the only way the Japanese might be made to surrender quickly."[13]

Although saving American lives was the main consideration, Truman saw other rationalizations for using the bomb. The air raids on Dresden and Tokyo in 1945, which had killed tens of thousands of Germans and Japanese, stood as precedents for doing with one bomb what thousands of planes had produced in these fire bombings or napalm attacks. Truman's initial understanding of the likely effects of the bomb suggested that it would not be all that much greater than the devastation caused by these earlier raids.[14] Nevertheless, he was entirely mindful of how terrifying the prospect of seeing their population centers destroyed one after another by atom bombs would be to the Japanese.

In addition, Truman could not ignore the fact that the decision to build the bomb at a cost of $2 billion had been Roosevelt's. If he had decided to rely on an invasion rather than atom bombs to force an end to the war, and this became public knowledge, he would have lost public confidence in his leadership and all that would mean for leading the nation for the next three years. He would have been seen as abandoning Roosevelt's agenda and giving in to sentimental concerns about saving the lives of Japanese civilians at a cost in American lives.

As Churchill understood it, there never was a decision to use the bomb. It was simply a given. "There never was a moment's discussion as to whether the atomic bomb should be used or not," he wrote later. "To avert a vast, indefinite butchery, to bring the war to an end, to give peace to the world, to lay healing hands upon its tortured peoples by a manifestation of overwhelming power at the cost of a few explosions, seemed, after all our toils and perils, a miracle of deliverance. . . . The decision whether or not to use the atomic bomb to compel the surrender of Japan was never even an issue." Agreement was "unanimous," Churchill concluded. He never heard "the slightest suggestion that we should do otherwise."[15]

In the end, Churchill had it right. The violence and death perpetrated by the Nazis and the Japanese, including the growing knowledge of Japanese atrocities committed against American and Filipino troops on the Bataan Death March and the concentration camps across Europe in which Hitler and his collaborators had ordered and implemented the destruction of six million Jews, fed a growing conviction that any devastation rained on the Germans and Japanese was nothing more than what they deserved. At Potsdam, recalled the American diplomat Charles Bohlen, the "spirit of mercy was not throbbing in the breast of any Allied official."[16]

Only in retrospect, after John Hersey's 1946 description of the suffering at Hiroshima initiated a fuller understanding of the destructiveness of nuclear weapons, did an outcry develop against Truman's decision to attack Hiroshima on August 6 and then Nagasaki on August 9 with atomic bombs that eventually killed perhaps as many as 150,000 civilians.

On August 10, Truman received a Japanese offer to surrender if the emperor could remain as head of state. Truman responded that Japan's proposal was acceptable, but that supreme authority in Japan would rest with the Allied occupation command. When the Japanese fell silent over the next three days, Truman assumed that the peace offer was a ploy and ordered a thousand-plane raid on Tokyo on August 13. The next day, Japanese radio read an address from the emperor accepting the Allied peace terms. Displays of ecstasy erupted in cities and towns across America.

The celebratory mood, however, was short-lived. The occupations of Germany and Japan seemed to go forward smoothly enough, but Soviet demands for a larger role in Japan's occupation provoked private tensions between Moscow and Washington. In September, a foreign ministers' meeting in London became an exercise in backbiting. Soviet resistance to Anglo-American pressure to relax their grip on Eastern and Southeastern Europe provoked remarks by Molotov suggesting fear that the United States might try to use the threat of an atomic attack to force Moscow's hand. "Of course, we all have to pay great attention to what Mr. Byrnes says," Molotov declared in a sarcastic toast to James Byrnes, who had succeeded Edward Stettinius as secretary of state in June, "because the United States are the only people who are making the atomic bomb."[17] When newspapers described the meeting as a failure, prospects for future peace seemed in jeopardy from deteriorating relations between the Soviet

Union and its former allies.

Difficulties became more pronounced in December at a second foreign ministers' conference in Moscow. The Soviets were as unyielding as ever on their control of Bulgaria, Romania, and Poland. In their East German occupation zone, they transferred territories to Poland as a way to diminish future German power and to compensate Poland for territories it had ceded to the Soviet Union. Furthermore, the Soviets would not consider proposals for free elections in Korea that would unify the country under one government. They feared losing control of the area north of the 38th parallel, where they had installed a Communist regime. Nor would they agree to withdraw troops from northern Iran, which the United States had declared an assault on that country's sovereignty.[18]

In a memo Truman gave Byrnes after the Moscow conference, he stated his determination to start taking a tougher line toward the Soviets. He described Romania and Bulgaria as "police states. I am not going to agree to the recognition of those governments unless they are radically changed. I think we ought to protest with all the vigor of which we are capable against the Russian program in Iran. It is also in line with the high-handed and arbitrary manner in which Russia acted in Poland. . . . There isn't a doubt in my mind that Russia intends an invasion of Turkey and the seizure of the Black Sea Straits to the Mediterranean. Unless Russia is faced with an iron fist and strong language another war is in the making. Only one language do they understand — 'how many divisions have you?' I do not think we should play compromise any longer. . . . I'm tired of babying the Soviets."[19]

International troubles were not confined to U.S.-Soviet tensions. In the fall of 1945, after Japan's surrender, China fell into a civil war. As long as the Chinese faced a common enemy in Japan, they managed to keep tensions between Chiang Kai-shek's Nationalist government and Mao Tse-tung's Communist Party in check. Once the war ended, however, these divisions immediately resurfaced. Roosevelt had tried to head off a postwar collision in China by signing agreements with Stalin at Yalta that seemed to ensure his support for a coalition government there. Stalin's price was Soviet control in Outer Mongolia; access to Dairen, China's warm-water port on the Kwantung peninsula; a lease on Manchuria's Port Arthur for use as a Soviet naval base; and shared control of Manchurian railways.[20]

Because neither Moscow nor Washington had the wherewithal to fully shape developments in China, a civil war erupted in the north in September, where the Communists were in control, and spread to other parts of the country in the fall. In November, Patrick Hurley, a Republican former secretary of war who had been serving as the U.S. ambassador to China, publicly announced his resignation without notifying the State Department or the White House. He compounded this slight to the president by declaring that the civil war was essentially the fault of U.S. Foreign Service officers in Chungking, who he said wanted to destroy Chiang's "corrupt, undemocratic" regime.[21]

The resignation and allegations incensed Truman, who privately told his cabinet, "See what a son-of-a-bitch did to me." The implication of Hurley's charge was that the president had allowed his subordinates to undermine Chiang and promote a Communist takeover in China. It was a transparent and damaging attack on the president's management of foreign policy and an opening Republican salvo against the White House and the Democrats in the 1946 congressional campaign.

To stop the fighting in China, Truman asked General George C. Marshall, the former army chief of staff, to replace Hurley as ambassador and negotiate an end to the civil war. Truman had the highest regard for Marshall as a military leader devoid of a partisan agenda. Although Marshall had recently retired, he selflessly agreed to assume what promised to be a thankless mission. His only condition on taking the assignment was that if mediation failed because of Chiang, Truman would nevertheless continue to back the Nationalists.

These developments in China, combined with the deterioration in Soviet-American relations, undermined the hopes of many Americans for a more placid world, and Truman's popularity suffered as cynicism about foreign affairs and isolationist sentiment resurfaced across the United States. But the erosion of the president's popularity had as much to do with domestic affairs as foreign affairs. Here again, Truman was operating in the long shadow of Franklin Roosevelt, who had led the country through the Depression and whose 1944 State of the Union message urged Americans not to be content if any segment of the nation was "ill-fed, ill-clothed, ill-housed, and insecure." He proposed an economic bill of rights that would assure every American of a job, food, clothing, housing, and adequate medical care.[22]

Just days after the formal Japanese surrender was signed on the deck of the USS *Missouri,* Truman echoed Roosevelt's call for economic security in a September 6 message to Congress that aimed to ensure a smooth transition from a wartime to a peacetime economy. His message reflected widespread national concerns that the end of the fighting, the reduced defense spending, and the need to absorb millions of demobilized troops into the labor force would lead to another Great Depression.[23] Truman well remembered the postwar slump in 1920 that cost him his haberdasher's shop, and many other Americans were equally worried. To guard against a serious economic downturn, Truman called for full employment legislation guaranteeing everyone a job at a good wage, fair employment practices to ensure against racial discrimination in hiring, affordable housing, aid to small businesses and farmers, a strengthened social security system, and a national health insurance program to protect Americans against the costs of serious illness.

In Congress, support for a new round of economic stimulus and social engineering was slim at best. Since 1938, when congressional elections had expanded the power of conservative Democrats, the New Deal had been stalled. Nothing in the post-1938 elections gave much reason to believe that the Congress and the country were ready to push beyond the economic and social reforms of the early New Deal years. Moreover, a series of strikes in the immediate postwar months fueled a national mood of conservatism. Labor unions were aggrieved at a falling standard of living for their members — reduced hours produced by an end to crash programs of war production and rising inflation caused by receding price controls and consumer shortages of everything from automobiles to housing eroded workers' purchasing power. Strikes, which impeded the production of scarce goods and added to the inflation, incensed middle-class Americans, who now saw unions as self-serving and unpatriotic. They wanted the government to step in and mediate union-industry disputes before there were work stoppages, or, if that failed, they favored arbitration to compel an end to strikes. A majority of Americans were unsympathetic or, at best, ambivalent about cost-of-living raises for workers, which seemed likely to drive up prices on such things as automobiles and housing.

Truman now found himself caught between the left and the right. "The storm of the war had passed," observed Robert J. Donovan, a historian of the Truman presidency. "But the turbulence in its wake, occasioned by the toils of simultaneously demobilizing the armed forces and reconverting the economy from wartime to peacetime production, all but capsized the Truman administration."[24] The president tried to keep the domestic peace by accommodating everyone or encouraging negotiated settlements among all factions and ended up satisfying no one.[25]

Although his September 6 message to Congress echoed Roosevelt's most progressive views, and the public saw Truman as leaning to the left in his domestic policies, particularly by pressing the case for universal national health insurance and a continuation of the Fair Employment Practices Commission, liberals were disappointed in him.[26] They did not feel that he was pressing Congress hard enough to enact his progressive agenda, though every astute political observer believed that White House pressure would do no good. In addition, liberals were angered by what they saw as the president's tepid support of labor.

Although he conceded that higher wages were essential to maintain national growth and prosperity, he saw union demands for 30 percent wage increases as excessive and certain to worsen inflation. He also gave his blessing to the establishment of fact-finding boards that could head off strikes, which labor leaders denounced as union busting.

His appointment of conservative Democrats to significant administration jobs also angered liberals. They were distressed by the selection of John W. Snyder, a Missouri banker and Truman "crony," to be the director of the Office of War Mobilization and Reconversion, where Snyder seemed certain to oppose government controls. They also objected to the selection of the California oilman Edwin Pauley, a conservative Democrat and outspoken opponent of Henry Wallace, as ambassador to the Allied Reparations Commission. Liberals saw Truman's affinity for party conservatives as symptomatic of his true economic and political leanings.[27]

Yet for all the liberals' complaints that Truman was too intent on limited government interference in the workings of the economy, he was still not especially palatable to American business leaders. The president's pressure on corporations to concede some wage increases to unions and his advocacy of what many conservatives described as Roosevelt's social welfare or socialist initiatives was enough to convince them that he was no ally of big business. Inflation eroding the purchasing power of all Americans and affordable housing in short supply raised questions among middle-class Americans about Truman's effectiveness in meeting the challenges of the postwar economy's conversion.

The problems that emerged in the last months of 1945 greatly distressed Truman. He had not wanted to be president, he repeatedly told associates at this time. "He says this to me practically every time that I see him and I wish that he wouldn't," noted Interior Secretary Harold Ickes. "The state of mind of which this is evidence is not good for him or for the country." In December, when Truman attended the Gridiron dinner, the annual gathering of Washington journalists at which they spoofed high government officials, Truman declared, only half in jest, that General William Tecumseh Sherman was wrong. It was not war but peace that is hell.[28]

Yet Truman, a keen student of American history, knew that being president meant shouldering heavy burdens. He could identify with George Washington's complaint that he "was beset by 'unmerited censures' of the vilest kind"; Thomas Jefferson's conclusion that the presidency was "a splendid misery"; Andrew Jackson's observation that the job was "a situation of dignified slavery"; James A. Garfield's lament, "What is there in this place that a man should ever want to get in to it?"; Woodrow Wilson's protest that "the president is a superior kind of slave"; Warren G. Harding's feeling that "this White House is a prison"; and Herbert Hoover's description of the office as "a compound hell."[29]

Truman would famously add to the list of complaints about the presidency by saying that it was like riding on the back of a tiger and that the White House was a big white jail or "the great white sepulcher of ambitions and reputations," as he described it to his wife, Bess.[30]

If the difficulties of his first eight months in the Oval Office had provoked doubts that the satisfactions of doing the job outweighed the frustrations, 1946 was to convince Truman that he would have been far better off remaining in the Senate, where he did not have to answer for every national problem, large and small, over which he had such limited control.

3
THE WORST OF TIMES

The year 1946 would test Harry Truman's stamina more than any of the many ordeals he had weathered in his twenty-four years in public life. The challenges of those twelve months gave added meaning to the novelist John Steinbeck's sympathetic observations about the ordeal of the presidency: "We give the President more work than a man can do, more responsibility than a man should take, more pressure than a man can bear. . . . We wear him out, use him up, eat him up. . . . He is ours and we exercise the right to destroy him."[1] Truman had no intention of letting any of the daily pressures overwhelm him. But he left no doubt that he saw himself in the eye of the storm when he famously accepted responsibility for all the country's tensions and woes by putting a sign on his desk that said, "The Buck Stops Here."[2]

The liberal columnist Max Lerner believed that Truman's travails were much the result of his own actions. Lerner granted that the transition from war to peace was no ordinary public burden, but he argued that Truman had made things especially hard on himself by trying to walk a middle ground on every issue of the day. Lerner called it Truman's "middle class mentality" or impulse "to blink the real social cleavage and struggles." Truman's appeals for "cooperation" were a failure of imagination. "In the end," Lerner argued, "you have to choose your side and fight on it."[3]

Truman took refuge in the understanding that most Americans wanted him to be a moderate leader holding to the center between ultraconservatives and ultraliberals. A Gallup survey in August 1945 found that 55 percent of respondents favored a middle-of-the-road course, in preference to movement by Truman to the left or right.[4]

It was not Truman's affinity for the center that made him so vulnerable to criticism but his tendency to compound his problems by being less than astute, at times, in anticipating public antagonism to some of his actions. His decision to make Ed Pauley undersecretary of the navy, for example, deepened skepticism on the Left about Truman's enthusiasm for party liberals.

Interior Secretary Harold Ickes, one of two prominent New Dealers left in the administration, attacked Pauley at a congressional hearing as unsuitable for the job. When Ickes resigned in February 1946 to protest Truman's insistence on sticking with Pauley, declaring himself opposed to "government by crony," his action increased liberal antagonism to the president.[5] This unfortunate political stumble on Truman's part opened him to ridicule: "To Err is Truman," conservatives began saying.[6]

Nevertheless, Truman's troubles were more the consequence of uncontrollable circumstances than the limitations of the man and his questionable leadership abilities. The journalist Richard Rovere believed that Truman's limited understanding of executive leadership was a serious problem for the new president and the country. But most of all, Rovere considered it "a cruel time to put inexperience in power."[7]

Truman's difficulties over demobilization of America's armed forces were a case in point. As the war came to an end in September 1945, Truman came under intense pressure to "bring the boys home." Where he saw a need to "adjust the rate of the demobilization of our forces so we would be able to meet our new obligations in the world," the public, led by the twelve million men in the armed forces and their families, insisted on the fastest possible release from service.[8] Because of serious doubts about the country's capability to establish effective occupations of Germany and Japan with diminished forces and its capacity to absorb so many men quickly into the economy, Truman was reluctant to give in to what he privately called the "disintegration of our armed forces."

Truman encouraged Congress to "take the heat" from a public insisting on rapid demobilization, which he privately told congressional leaders could jeopardize global stability. He wanted them to encourage a more measured return of the most deserving or longest-serving troops rather than an indiscriminate release of most of the boys. Congress, which was inundated with pleas from wives demanding the return of husbands for the sake of their fatherless children, was no help. One member of the House warned that Congress would find itself in "the hottest water," as it "ought to be," if it did not expedite the release of servicemen who had fulfilled their patriotic duty.[9]

Although a presidential appeal to an America mindful that it could not shun its new international obligations might have relieved some of the pressure for a rapid demobilization, Truman refused to confront the public with an unpopular demand. Opinion polls showed that most Americans might have been open to a presidential appeal: the public understood that atomic bombs would not be enough to ensure the peace, favored congressional renewal of the existing draft law, and supported the president's proposal for compulsory military training for all able-bodied young men for a year to eighteen months.[10] And yet Truman was disinclined to confront the country with the emerging dangers he saw from Soviet aggression, which would have been the implicit argument for maintaining a significant part of the national force in the postwar period. He feared that such a frank appeal might have heightened international tensions and encouraged resurgent isolationism. On the other hand, demobilization had its attractions. A smaller military would make it easier for Truman to reduce the budget deficits that were spurring inflation.

Despite his hesitation about pressing the country for a commitment that could provoke strong opposition, international developments by January 1946 compelled him to announce his unwillingness "to discharge every member of the armed forces promptly." He declared that "the future of our country . . . [is] now as much at stake as it was in the days of the war."[11] His announcement touched off an explosion of hostility, including demonstrations at American military bases around the globe, where servicemen were waiting to be shipped home. The protesters' slogan was "No boats, No votes." At a press conference, the journalist Drew Pearson tried to hand Truman a stack of soldiers' petitions asking their release from service. In what was not his finest moment, the president refused to accept them and threatened to punch Pearson in the nose for a falsehood he had broadcast on the radio about his wife and daughter's travel from Independence to Washington in a private railway car.[12]

Truman's call for slower demobilization, however, could not overcome the pressures by war veterans for an end to military service. As a result, in the spring of 1946, he had to ask Congress to extend the Selective Service law for another year, which it agreed to do in response to pressure from U.S. military chiefs.

Universal military training, however, was another matter. Truman urged Congress to act on what he believed was essential to the country's future security by enacting a law requiring military service for all able-bodied young men. But Truman's diminished credibility in the military sphere, coupled with behind-the-scenes opposition from the navy, undermined his chances of winning a positive congressional response.[13]

By March 1946, *Collier's* magazine featured an article on "Truman's Troubled Year" that he kept on his desk to show visitors as perhaps an implicit plea not to add to his burdens.[14] The alienation of liberals over the Ickes-Pauley flap and veterans' families over the pace of demobilization were only two of the problems that had thrown the president on the defensive. The whole domestic scene — economic and social conflicts — confronted him with hard choices that left few Americans satisfied with the direction of national affairs.

Labor unions were a constant source of presidential grief. In a nationally broadcast speech on January 3, Truman lamented the rising "industrial strife" in almost every major industry and the potential for runaway inflation that could precipitate "a crash that will be much more serious than 1920." He described the stakes for 1946 as very high: "This year we lay the foundation for our economic structure which will have to serve for generations."[15]

Although he put the greatest blame for the country's industrial tensions on Congress's failure to enact the economic program he had proposed the previous September, privately he was angry at labor, management, and the public for putting selfish needs above the larger national interest. "A superman cannot successfully meet world problems in this age without the help of the people," he complained in comments to himself that never found their way into his speech. He described labor as making "power crazy demands" reminiscent of "arrogant industry" in the 1920s. Management, which wouldn't "meet the situation halfway," was just as bad.[16]

When 800,000 steelworkers walked off the job in mid-January — the biggest work stoppage in the country's history — and automobile workers, glassmakers, telephone operators, electric utilities employees, and numerous other industrial laborers struck in protest against inadequate wages, fringe benefits, and working conditions, Truman had no effective response other than pleas to both sides to consider the broader needs of the nation. The steel strike would be settled in February, but the agreement was seen as certain to stimulate additional inflation that in time would provoke unions to make new wage demands.

In April and May, a coal strike that forced shutdowns in other industries was followed by a national rail workers stoppage that disrupted transportation all over the country. A majority of Americans now decisively favored laws forbidding all strikes in "public service industries such as electric, gas, telephone, and local transportation companies." Seventy percent of the country supported a moratorium on "all strikes and lockouts for a year." Truman was so incensed by the indifference of the railway unions to the national interest that he asked Congress in a speech in the House to pass a law that allowed him "to draft into the Armed Forces of the United States all workers who are on strike against their government."[17] His personal appearance underscored the importance he put on the suggested legislation.

Although the House promptly agreed to his request, despite news that the railroad unions had accepted a settlement, the Senate rejected the president's plea as allowing an unconstitutional expansion of presidential authority that the country would regret in the future. Harold Ickes called Truman's bill "the heaviest blow ever struck in

America against the fundamental rights of labor and the democratic traditions of our country."[18] Although Truman would win a boost in public approval from his dramatic call for draconian measures against "selfish" workers acting so indifferently to the public good, it was only temporary.

Substantial majorities also faulted the president's ineffectiveness in controlling inflation. After Truman had loosened price controls on some manufactured goods and food (especially meat, which was in short supply), gasoline, and clothes, prices shot up in an inflationary spiral that threatened the country's economic stability. Although Truman revisited the problem as inflation mounted in 1946, calling for an extension of the Office of Price Administration, which was due to expire in June, he had lost public trust on managing the economy.[19]

By this point, the press's assessments of the president's leadership were almost uniformly negative. *The Nation* characterized Truman as a "weak, baffled, angry man."[20] Walter Lippmann, America's most famous columnist, decried Truman's decision to surround himself with men whose questionable judgments made them more a deterrent than a help in reaching wise decisions. Others faulted Truman for being excessively "indecisive" and "vacillating," a president without a clear sense of purpose or too willing to accommodate himself to conflicting points of view in hopes of satisfying everyone or alienating no one. The *New York Herald Tribune* described New Dealers as "unhappy," conservatives as "critical," and moderates or independents as "uncertain" about the president. "I'm just mild about Harry," went a current Washington joke.[21]

All this criticism frustrated and angered Truman. But he hid his irritation, expressing his annoyance in private comments or speeches he wrote not for public delivery but as a way to ventilate his hostility toward critics. In the privacy of the Oval Office, he described the people closest to Roosevelt as "crackpots and the lunatic fringe." He told Julius Krug, Ickes's replacement as secretary of the interior, that perhaps he should appoint a secretary of columnists, who would read all the editorials and opinion articles in the newspapers and then tell him how the country should be run. A draft speech he wrote during the railroad strike included a satiric proposal for hanging a few traitors. In the fall of 1946, when the public turned against a continuation of price controls, he privately denounced his constituents for "following Mammon instead of Almighty God," for having "gone over to the powers of selfishness and greed."[22]

At the time, Truman took refuge in the belief that no one else had effective answers to the problems he was facing. But he was rationalizing his own limitations. The country was indeed beset by unexpected difficulties. Held fast by the recent experience with the Depression and memories of the economic downturn after World War I, most everyone, including Truman, expected the immediate post-1945 period to replicate or approximate those earlier crashes. So when inflation and strikes became the principal economic problems, neither Truman nor his advisers were ready with an effective response. Moreover, as someone still feeling his way in the presidency, Truman was unsure of himself and unprepared to offer clear leadership, which only made the problems appear larger.

In later writings after he left office, Truman expressed sympathy for Herbert Hoover, "who did the best he possibly could but was faced with difficulties that he just wasn't able to overcome at the time. I think he and his administration were blamed for things that were not their fault."[23] If he were willing to give Hoover and himself the benefit of the doubt in struggling with insurmountable economic problems, he also came to see that effectiveness in a crisis required "a president who can make up his own mind, who isn't afraid of controversy" or of offending groups opposed to his actions. He concluded that "our country has never suffered seriously from any acts of the president that were truly intended for the welfare of the country; it's suffered from the inaction of a great many presidents when action should have been taken at the right time. He has to keep reminding people that a good president must do more than just believe in what he says — he must also act on what he believes."

Although he didn't acknowledge the connection to his 1946 travails, he surely had them in mind when he later wrote that a weak president "can't control things; if he isn't, then he can meet the situation . . . by getting the people who really count to go along with him. Reasonable people will always go along with a man who has the right ideas and leadership."

Difficulties abroad matched Truman's problems at home. In February, Joseph Stalin announced a new Five-Year Plan with a warning to Soviet citizens that they would have to sacrifice consumer goods to military might, which would be essential in a coming confrontation with the capitalist, imperialist West. Many Americans saw the speech as tantamount to a declaration of war, which Stalin seemed to think was inevitable. Two weeks later, newspaper reports of Soviet agents in Canada funneling atomic secrets to Moscow aroused fears that Communist sympathizers in the United States government were engaged in espionage that would speed Soviet development of atomic weapons in preparation for an all-out conflict with America and its allies.[24]

Some in the United States, led by former vice president Henry Wallace — now serving as Truman's secretary of commerce — believed that the spying and Stalin's speech were defensive reactions to American belligerence, especially Washington's refusal to offer Moscow a generous reconstruction loan.[25] But others in the American government were increasingly convinced of Soviet determination to undermine the United States at home and abroad in a contest for world dominance. George F. Kennan, the American chargé d'affaires in Moscow, gave forceful expression to this fear in what became known as the "long telegram" of February 22, 1946.[26] A Russian expert and longtime observer of Soviet affairs, Kennan warned that there was no way to disarm Soviet hostility toward the West: it was the product of a need to consolidate power at home by arousing fears of unrelenting foreign dangers. The West needed to resist Communist expansion and attempts at subversion of democratic institutions, he argued, while waiting until Soviet rule collapsed because of its own internal contradictions.

Truman read and approved of Kennan's analysis and prescription for dealing with the Soviet threat. But domestic political crosscurrents made him loath to say so openly. When a journalist at a February 21 press conference had asked the president if in view of "current revelations" about Soviet aggressiveness, he still "didn't share the unholy fear of Russia," as he had said several months earlier, Truman replied, "No comment."

His caution was as much in evidence two weeks later, when he accompanied Winston Churchill to give a speech at Westminster College in Fulton, Missouri. Churchill had described the contents of his speech to the president beforehand and gave a copy to Truman to read on the train. Truman told the former prime minister that "it was admirable and would do some good." Truman further put his stamp on Churchill's remarks by introducing him to the Westminster College audience. Churchill's speech left no doubt that he was urging Washington to take the lead in an anti-Soviet coalition: "From Stettin in the Baltic to Trieste in the Adriatic," Churchill famously declared, "an Iron Curtain has descended across the continent. Behind that line lie all the capitals of the ancient states of central and eastern Europe" that had fallen under Soviet control. Churchill then advocated an Anglo-American military alliance that could act as an effective check on Soviet expansionism.[27]

Despite Truman's tacit public approval of Churchill's speech, administration spokesmen denied the president's advance knowledge or endorsement of the prime minister's remarks. Concern that open backing might provoke a crisis in Soviet-American relations persuaded Truman to hide his satisfaction at Churchill's warning and call for action.

Domestic pressures likewise made Truman reluctant to identify his administration with Churchill's warning about Soviet intentions. Walter Lippmann called Churchill's speech an "almost catastrophic blunder" that would increase the likelihood of an East-West war.[28] Critical comments also followed from liberals, including Eleanor Roosevelt, Harold Ickes, and Henry Wallace, who labeled the speech an attack on Moscow and the call for an Anglo-American alliance a slight to the United Nations.[29] Truman was leery of taking a public stance that might antagonize a significant part of his party's base, and he also doubted whether Americans, however sympathetic to strong public criticism of Soviet behavior, were ready to sign on to tough policies, including a strengthened military, which might intimidate Moscow.

Truman's reluctance to take an open stand on Churchill's remarks — neither criticizing them nor openly aligning himself with them — further undermined his public standing. "It was a bad time for Truman," observes David McCullough. "To the press and an increasing proportion of the country, he seemed bewildered and equivocating, incapable of a clear or positive policy toward the Russians."[30]

Even when Truman put a foot right, he received no credit for it. In March, when a deadline passed for a promised Soviet withdrawal of its troops from Iran's northern province of Azerbaijan (where Moscow had stationed troops during the war), the

State Department, led by Secretary of State Byrnes, publicly endorsed UN demands for an end to Soviet violations of Iranian sovereignty. Although a Soviet withdrawal was greeted with satisfaction in the United States, especially by officials who saw this as a successful demonstration of Kennan's containment strategy, Byrnes and the UN received praise for the diplomatic victory, rather than Truman, who had put private pressure on Stalin for a withdrawal.[31]

Where there was failure, however, the blame fell on the president. A case in point was when the State Department developed a proposal to limit the spread of atomic weapons, for presentation to the United Nations Atomic Energy Commission. The proposal, written by Dean Acheson, the undersecretary of state, and David Lilienthal, the Tennessee Valley Authority chairman, called for national commitments against building atomic bombs and the elimination of the U.S. atomic arsenal should it seem certain that other countries would not construct such weapons. The Acheson-Lilienthal proposal aimed to ensure support in Congress and the public by maintaining America's atomic monopoly until it was clear that the United States could jettison its arsenal without risk to its national security. Acheson and Lilienthal hoped to win Soviet backing by reposing trust in Moscow's self-denying commitment without insistence on international inspections of Soviet territory.

Because Byrnes and Truman remained concerned that Congress would object to any agreement eliminating America's freedom to sustain its international military dominance with atomic weapons, they enlisted the participation of the financier Bernard Baruch, whose political influence was strong among Democrats and Republicans alike. Baruch agreed to represent the United States at the UN commission's deliberations, but only on the condition that the U.S. proposal be identified as his and not the State Department's and that he be free to alter some of its provisions. Specifically, he insisted on including sanctions against any nation violating the arms control agreement and the suspension of the Security Council veto of potential sanctions, meaning that Moscow would not be able to prevent UN action against it if it broke a promise not to build the bomb.

Truman felt compelled to appease Baruch, who was a prima donna with a flair for public dramatics: when he introduced what was now called the Baruch Plan at the UN, he announced the world organization faced a choice between "the quick and the dead."

Neither the U.S. Congress nor Moscow was comfortable with the proposal, which died after months of deliberations at the UN. Consequently, Truman won no approval from conservatives, who considered the whole idea a prescription for appeasing the Soviet Union, or from liberals, who denounced the plan as a sham proposal calculated to ensure America's continued monopoly of atomic weapons and an additional provocation to the Soviets, who saw it as a way to ensure America's military superiority.

Moscow's rejection of the Baruch Plan incensed Truman, and at one point he expressed his increasing anti-Soviet sentiments in Henry Wallace's presence — which in turn frightened Wallace into thinking that Truman's intemperateness toward the Soviet Union might lead to a third world war.

Wallace tried to encourage Truman to be more understanding of the Soviets' point of view. He told the president that the country's suffering in World War II, coupled with acts of perceived American bellicosity, were frightening Moscow and provoking tensions that could lead to a conflict. Truman was not convinced. He saw Wallace as a well-meaning eccentric with little knowledge of world affairs and poor judgment in particular about Soviet intentions. By September, Truman had begun to see the Russians as acting ruthlessly in their self-interest, which included undermining an America they considered a deadly adversary. He remained hopeful, nevertheless, that checking Soviet expansionism would lead not to war but to a standoff competition in which the United States would ultimately prevail.[32]

The Truman-Wallace differences over Soviet-American relations came to a head on September 12, when Wallace gave a speech at Madison Square Garden in New York, which was billed as a political address supporting Democratic candidates in the November congressional elections. Instead, Wallace took the opportunity to focus on American foreign policy and the requirements for future peace. Specifically, he spoke out against the administration's recent expressions of determination to "get tough with Russia." He warned that the Soviets would match all American moves in this direction. "We must not let our Russian policy be guided or influenced by those inside or outside the United States who want war with Russia," he said.

Wallace had reviewed the speech with

Truman in a face-to-face meeting at the White House, during which the president voiced no objections. Moreover, at a press conference on the afternoon of the twelfth, reporters, who had an advance copy of Wallace's remarks, asked the president's reaction. Truman answered, "I approved the whole speech." When asked if he considered Wallace's statements at odds with what Byrnes had been saying about Russia, Truman replied, "I do not. They are exactly in line."

Before Wallace gave his speech, at least two members of the administration warned the president and others in the White House that it would embarrass him, because it contradicted Byrnes's anti-Soviet pronouncements and made the president seem as if he was going in two different directions at once. In short, it would be a confirmation of Truman's uncertain leadership.

Yet Truman let Wallace go ahead with his speech. Speculation abounds that he was altogether too casual about what Wallace would say and that his inattentiveness and remarks to the press raised additional doubts about his capacity to serve as president. The dispute did indeed raise questions about Truman's inconsistency, and the resignation provoked outrage among liberals, who echoed Wallace's accusations that Truman was recklessly leading the country into an unnecessary war with the Soviet Union.

But one can also read what happened as Truman's design for ridding himself of Wallace, who was increasingly at odds with his view of the Soviet danger. When he told the press that Wallace's speech was in line with administration pronouncements on Moscow, he may well have been creating an opportunity to complain to the press later on that Wallace's actual remarks were a departure from what he assumed they would be, despite knowing full well what he would say. An effective president needed to be "a liar" and "double-crosser," Truman told his daughter in a letter about the Wallace affair. In a diary note, Truman decried Wallace's desire "to disband our armed forces and trust a bunch of adventurers in the Kremlin Politbureau." He described Wallace and "the Reds, phonies, and 'parlor pinks' " as "a national danger."

Truman's public opposition to Wallace's remarks forced Wallace to resign as secretary of commerce, and Truman was happy to see him go. Truman told his mother and sister, "Well, now he's out, and the crackpots are having conniption fits. I'm glad they are. It convinces me I'm right."[33]

However successful the maneuver in getting rid of Wallace, it did nothing to help the Democratic Party in the November elections. To the contrary, it cemented the feeling among liberal Democrats that Truman's caution and ineptitude had decisively separated him from Roosevelt, killed the New Deal, and set the country on a road to war with a frightened Soviet Union. Conservative southern Democrats were equally alienated from the president for a Fair Employment Practices Committee aimed at promoting equal opportunity for blacks and continuing federal government controls through the Office of Price Administration and over offshore oil, which put the president at odds with southern states claiming they, and not the federal government, controlled the oil rights.

If Democrats were discouraged about going to the polls, Republicans were full of hope that they could recapture control of Congress for the first time since 1930. One Ohio congressman reflected the mood of the country when he described national frustrations over consumer shortages of housing and meat, inflation, strikes, and the Communist threat at home and abroad. A Boston advertising agency working for the

Republican National Committee brilliantly summed up the national eagerness for change with the question: "Had Enough?" The committee's chairman added to the attack a description of the Democratic Party as made up of "southern racists, big-city bosses, and radicals bent on 'Sovietizing' the country." Republican congressional candidates shamelessly identified Democratic opponents as being in league with Communists or naively trusting of Russia, as they complained Roosevelt had been of Stalin at Yalta, enabling the Soviet Union to seize control of Eastern Europe.

The election results were a decisive defeat for the Democrats and Truman's stewardship. The Republicans won a fifty-eight-seat margin in the House, 246 to 188, and a six-seat advantage in the Senate. Among the Republican newcomers were Senator Joseph McCarthy of Wisconsin and Representative Richard Nixon of California. Among the smaller number of Democratic freshmen was a twenty-nine-year-old navy veteran from Massachusetts named John F. Kennedy.[34]

Familiar with political setbacks in his career, Truman was philosophical about the defeat. "To be president of the United States is to be lonely, very lonely at times of great decisions," he said. "Lincoln had fits of melancholy," he reminded himself. "Melancholy goes with the job." In his moments of greatest discouragement, he gave in to despair and self-pity: "I am in a position that's too big for me. In fact I think it's too big for anybody but I know it's too big for me. I need help, help, help." He added: "A man in his right mind would never want to be president if he knew what it entails. Aside from the impossible administrative burden, he has to take all sorts of abuse from liars and demagogues."

Yet, characteristically, he quickly bounced back and declared himself ready to fight for what he believed right for the country. When Congressman J. William Fulbright of Arkansas, a former Rhodes scholar, said that Truman should appoint the Republican senator Arthur Vandenberg of Michigan as secretary of state and then resign as a prelude to making Vandenberg president, Truman dismissed Fulbright as "Halfbright." "Nobody but a damn fool would have the job in the first place," Truman also said. "But I've got it damn fool or no and I have to do it as best I can."

After months of equivocation about how to proceed in dealing with the conflicting demands on him for one policy or another, an indecisiveness that had contributed to his 1946 defeats, the election losses provoked a new mind-set in the president. He decided to stop trying to be all things to all people: "I think the proper thing to do . . . is to do what I think is right and let them all go to hell." Truman press secretary Charlie Ross caught the new mood in the White House when he wrote his sister: "The consensus is that President Truman is now a free man and can write a fine record in the coming two years."[35] It was a strikingly accurate prediction.

4
POLITICIAN AND
STATESMAN

In his postelection ruminations on his party's defeat, Truman told Bess that he was determined to act "in all cases . . . without regard to political considerations, what seems to me to be for the welfare of all our people."[1] It was a noble sentiment, which reflected his honest concern for the national well-being. But, like all professional politicians, he was convinced that his policies would serve the country better than those of his opponents, which meant doing what he believed would ensure his political survival. And that in turn meant winning popular approval: "The president is helpless unless he is backed by public opinion," he told a group of civil rights advocates in 1946.[2]

With two years to go before he would have to face voters, Truman believed he had time for a comeback. But he could not wait to repair his public standing. He needed at once to find common ground with a majority of Americans; any hesitation or equivocation about identifying himself with popular sentiment could make it all the harder to repair the political damage.

He found the perfect foil in John L. Lewis, the president of the United Mine Workers union. Lewis was a gruff, overbearing, and uncompromising advocate of the miners who prided himself on having stood up to presidents in pursuit of his members' interests. When he got into a labor dispute with New York's mayor Fiorello La Guardia, he dismissively told him, "We don't take any stuff off the President of the United States and we're not taking any off you, Mr. Mayor."[3]

Roosevelt and Truman both despised Lewis, whom they saw as more concerned with the needs of his union than those of the country. In 1943, when he threatened a coal strike that could undermine the war effort, Roosevelt asked China's Madame Chiang Kai-shek, who was staying at the White House, how her husband's government would deal with such a labor leader in wartime. When she expressively drew a finger across her throat, Roosevelt exploded in laughter.[4] For his part, Truman privately described Lewis as a "racketeer" and a "son of a bitch."[5]

The public shared this contempt for Lewis; in a May 1946 Gallup poll, only 13 percent of Americans had a favorable opinion of him, while 69 percent had negative feelings. As 1946 ended, Americans saw control of strikes as the country's greatest problem, and 50 percent of a poll favored a law suspending strikes and lockouts for a year.[6]

In December 1946, when Lewis threatened a new walkout of the mines, which were being run by the government after seizing them the previous spring, Truman was determined to use a clash with Lewis not only to head off a damaging blow to the economy but also to serve his political ends. Refusing to talk to Lewis and forcing the dispute with the UMW into the courts, the president was able to win an injunction against a strike. When Lewis defied the court and ordered a work stoppage, Truman won a contempt citation against him. Lewis then called off the strike with the explanation that he would wait for a Supreme Court decision to resolve the conflict, but the press and the public saw the outcome as a clear victory for the president, who was now celebrated as the one man in America with the guts to face down John L. Lewis.[7]

Privately, Truman congratulated himself on having "whipped a damned traitor." Truman's approval rating jumped 13 points, from 35 percent to 48 percent.[8]

The loyalty of federal employees was an equally inviting popular political issue that Truman felt he couldn't ignore. During the 1946 elections, the reports about the Canadian spy ring had moved Republicans to attack the Democrats for making America vulnerable to Communist subversion by coddling ultraliberal, pro-Soviet government officials. By the summer of 1946, large majorities of Americans were convinced that the Soviet Union had spies at work in the United States and that Communist Party members should be barred from civil service jobs.

Truman assumed that a Republican Congress would exploit these public fears by investigations aimed more at Democrats than at the handful of Communists who actually held or were applying for government jobs. Anyone knowledgeable about the Red scare following World War I or familiar with the aggressive current attacks on dissenters by the House Un-American Activities Committee shared the president's concern that anticommunism had become more of a political bludgeon than a realistic campaign to preserve American institutions.[9] Congressman Richard Nixon's successful 1946 campaign, in which he attacked his Democratic opponent, Jerry Voorhis, as a Communist sympathizer, was an example of how vulnerable liberals could be to charges of fellow traveling or Communist connections.

In November, Truman created the President's Temporary Commission on Employee Loyalty, none of whose six members was notable for his sensitivity to civil liberties. They were tasked to study the procedures for assessing the loyalty of current and potential government workers. The commission was as much a political device for blunting mounting anti-Communist fears undermining confidence in the Truman administration as a national security tool for preserving the American way of life.

When the new Congress convened in January 1947, it quickly became evident that it would be an instrument for turning aside liberal reforms and a Republican launching pad for a 1948 anti-Truman presidential campaign. Dominated by conservative midwestern and western Republicans such as Robert Taft of Ohio, Kenneth Wherry of Nebraska, and William Knowland of California as well as racist southern

Democrats such as Mississippi's Senator James O. Eastland and Congressman John Rankin, the Republicans, as Robert Donovan noted, took pains to denounce the New Deal, which was "un-American" and "unconstitutional."

Wherry was emblematic of the parochial outlook common to so many members of his party: their world was divided between good and evil, and their ignorance of foreign affairs was captured in Wherry's description of Southeast Asia as "Indigo China."[10] In their view, Truman was Roosevelt's heir, who would use the presidency to perpetuate liberal abuses of power and allow Communists to take over the world.

No two issues unified conservatives on both sides of the aisle as much as anticommunism and reining in unpopular labor unions. As demonstrated by his willingness to establish a study commission on government worker loyalty, Truman felt compelled to follow through in March on his commission's call for stronger measures to ensure against Communist infiltration of the federal government. In the hope of heading off more aggressive investigations by right-wing congressmen, Truman issued an executive order establishing a Federal Employees Loyalty and Security Program.

According to Clark Clifford, the White House counsel, Truman had little concern about Communist subversion in the government. "It was a political problem," Clifford said. "Truman was going to run in '48, and that was it. . . . The President didn't attach fundamental importance to the so-called Communist scare. He thought it was a lot of baloney. But political pressures were such that he had to recognize it." Clifford saw the complaints about disloyalty as a manufactured problem.

Sadly, the program exposed civil servants to anonymous attacks based not on hard evidence but on what accusers described as "reasonable grounds" of their "disloyalty," which was left undefined in the executive order. Nor did the order provide federal employees under suspicion with the chance to confront their accusers or even know the evidence against them.

It was a program that did nothing to serve national security. Between 1947 and 1951, several thousand employees resigned under a cloud, and 212 were dismissed, but no one was ever indicted and no evidence of espionage was ever uncovered. Truman accurately foresaw that the program might produce arbitrary abuses, but he was so worried that doing nothing would lead to even greater misuse of power by a paranoid Congress and a repressive FBI he compared to the "Gestapo" that he put his own investigative machinery in place. It was more a sad commentary on the politics of the moment than on what Truman did to maintain some semblance of control over the anti-Communist hysteria. Truman himself later characterized his actions as "terrible."[11]

Though Truman gave in to the pressures of the moment about fears of domestic spying and subversion, he would not follow the congressional lead in limiting the rights of labor unions. A central preoccupation of the Eightieth Congress was to meet public pressure for a revision of the National Labor Relations Act of 1935, which had legalized collective bargaining and exempted unions from antitrust laws that courts had used to prohibit strikes.

The provisions of a bill named for Senator Taft and New Jersey representative Fred Hartley Jr., who chaired the Senate and House labor committees, sharply curtailed union rights. The closed shop, a requirement that a new employee belong to a union, could be prohibited by state right-to-work laws; union members had to sign non-Communist affidavits; unions could not make political contributions and could be sued in federal courts for contract violations; and presidents could act in an emergency to delay and impede a strike. Both the Senate and the House passed the Taft-Hartley Act in June 1947 by veto-proof margins.

Truman came under intense pressure from labor and liberal Democrats to reject the law and leave it to a conservative Congress to reenact it over his veto. He thought Taft-Hartley was a bad law. Although pressed by all but two members of his cabinet to sign it and understanding that the measure reflected a national majority's desire to rein in unions, he rejected it as "burdensome, arbitrary, unnecessary, and unwarranted." In a radio address, he told the nation that it was "bad for labor, bad for management, and bad for the country." He added, "We do not need — and we do not want — legislation which will take fundamental rights away from our working people."

Truman's daughter, Margaret, later wrote that "while he was responding to his presidential conscience, my father did not by any means stop being a politician. The two are by no means incompatible." It was an accurate description of his veto decision. He not only considered the law an overdrawn reaction to unions but he also saw a chance to repair some of the damage he had suffered among liberals when Ickes and Wallace had broken with him and he had agreed to a potentially repressive loyalty program. Although the Congress, with conservative southern Democrats joining Republicans, easily overrode the president's veto, Truman won renewed political backing from labor and liberals more generally, many of whom now pledged to back him in 1948.[12]

The president also received a boost in popularity from a bold foreign policy initiative — the Truman Doctrine.

The doctrine was the product of evolving American fears of Soviet expansionism. Moscow's aggressiveness in making Eastern Europe a sphere of influence had provoked Kennan's long telegram of February 1946 and Churchill's Iron Curtain speech in March. Soviet moves in the summer to pressure Turkey into shared defense of the Black Sea straits had persuaded Truman to increase America's naval presence in the eastern Mediterranean and to make clear to Moscow that the United States objected to demands on Ankara for a Soviet role in policing a Turkish sea-lane. It was a cautionary warning to the Soviet Union against trying to expand its influence in the Near East, which Moscow could use to threaten Middle East oil supplies and support Communist parties in Western Europe.

Where Kennan's telegram and the tensions over Turkey were largely unpublished government exchanges that stirred no clear public response, Churchill's pronouncement had touched off a domestic debate in the United States. American sentiment had turned decidedly against the Soviet government, which a majority in the United States now saw as intent on world control. But many in the country, especially on the left, held out hopes for the conciliatory diplomacy they associated with Franklin Roosevelt to reestablish wartime cooperation between East and West.

Others in the United States were less sure but were not ready to endorse immediate militant action to block expanding Soviet power. They saw domestic Communists as a problem, but a government loyalty program and the banning of the party from participation in domestic politics could blunt that danger, or so most believed. In short, Americans, including the new Republican Congress, were on edge but not ready to commit resources to prevent or guard the country against the prospect of a Soviet move toward European or world domination.

Nor had Truman been willing to make that case to the public before two of his principal aides gave him a lengthy report in the summer of 1946 on the threat of Soviet aggression and, more important, the growing danger of a Communist takeover in Greece. In February 1947, the British government informed Washington that strains on its economy from postwar shortages and the worst winter weather in decades now compelled London to end its aid to Turkey and to withdraw its troops from Greece, where it had been supporting an anti-Communist government. Britain's departure from the eastern Mediterranean, the State Department advised the president, left a power vacuum that the Soviets would be all too likely to fill. It could also be a prelude to expanded Communist influence in Italy and France and more general Soviet control of Europe.

The president did not need convincing. His problem was how to persuade Congress and the American people that the United States must once again protect the national interest by coming to the defense of Europe. More specifically, he needed to convince Americans that the Soviet threat was more than an abstraction and that financial and material support to Greece and Turkey were the keys to blunting a Communist offensive.

In a White House meeting with congressional leaders on February 27, Truman asked George Marshall, who had succeeded James Byrnes as secretary of state that month, to make the case for aid to Greece and Turkey. Although Marshall had failed to negotiate a lasting truce in China, where the continuing civil war threatened to bring the Communist Party to power, he was in no way tainted by the collapse of his mediation efforts. His standing as one of the architects of military victory in World War II gave him exceptional clout with Congress, which approved his appointment as secretary without dissent. His reputation as a nonpartisan patriot, who sacrificed his personal comfort to serve in China and now further as secretary of state, made him the ideal official to plead the case for aid to Greece and Turkey.

Marshall's presentation received a respectful hearing on Capitol Hill, but it was more a soldier's factual statement than an impassioned plea for a costly commitment that could win an instant positive response from skeptical congressmen and senators. When Dean Acheson, the undersecretary of state, followed Marshall with a dramatic call to arms that frightened the leaders into seeing a clear and present danger, Michigan senator Arthur Vandenberg, a recent Republican convert to internationalism, declared himself ready to support Truman's request and was confident that others would join in if he made it directly to a joint congressional session. The senator shrewdly understood that it would take a forceful warning about the Communist danger for the president to overcome congressional resistance to spending additional money on foreign aid of any kind.

Truman understood that his request to help Greece and Turkey represented much more than a new overseas expenditure but a dramatic step away from old-fashioned isolationism and toward a new internationalism or a demonstration of America's enduring commitments abroad. To his credit, he also understood that the United States could not be everywhere and did not have unlimited resources to provide financial and military support in every corner of the globe. In China, for instance, where civil war was now raging, Truman had no thoughts of involving the United States in an open-ended commitment to Chiang Kaishek's corrupt government. A land war in

Asia against a Communist insurgency impressed him as an unwise expenditure of scarce U.S. resources. He knew that neither the Congress nor the public was prepared to fight in China, however much they favored blunting Communist expansion.

In his speech to Congress on March 12, Truman characterized the crisis as part of a larger contest between freedom and totalitarianism. "Totalitarian regimes imposed upon free peoples, by direct or indirect aggression, undermine the foundations of international peace and hence the security of the United States," he said. "I believe that it must be the policy of the United States to support free people who are resisting attempted subjugation by armed minorities or by outside pressures."[13]

The president's request for $400 million to aid Greece and Turkey did not meet with universal approval. While Truman's appeal struck responsive chords in the Congress, which agreed to the funding, and 56 percent of a poll supported Truman's request to help Greece, almost two-thirds of the country preferred to have the United Nations take responsibility for the crisis in the Near East.

The columnist Walter Lippmann supported a limited aid program but objected to "a vague global policy which sounds like the tocsin of an ideological crusade" with "no limits."[14] He worried about the long-term effects. The historian John L. Gaddis later echoed the point: Truman presented "aid to Greece and Turkey in terms of an ideological conflict between two ways of life" and "encouraged a simplistic view of the Cold War which was, in time, to imprison American diplomacy in an ideological straitjacket almost as confining as that which restricted Soviet foreign policy."[15] In short, although Truman's appeal would achieve its immediate purposes, it would make it difficult for later presidents to pursue steps toward a less belligerent policy and détente with international communism.

In June, Marshall raised the stakes on the scope of America's commitment to Europe. Speaking for the Truman administration in a commencement address at Harvard, Marshall set forth a plan for repairing the devastated economies of all European nations. The plan was brilliantly conceived. The State Department decided against proposing outright financial grants, structuring instead a European-wide cooperative effort to use American funds to repair national economies. The Soviets and their Eastern European satellites were not to be excluded from the program but were invited to participate. This was done to ensure against charges that aid exclusively given to Western Europe would promote a deeper East-West divide. As Marshall would say in his Harvard address, "Our policy is directed not against any country or doctrine, but against hunger, poverty, desperation and chaos. Its purpose should be the revival of a worldwide working economy promoting the survival of free institutions." If the Communist bloc countries chose not to take part in the U.S.-financed plan, the burden of dividing the continent would fall on them.

To sell the program to Congress, the emphasis needed to be on European initiatives to fix their own economies rather than on the United States to do it for them. Having already provided some $6 billion in postwar aid, which was proving insufficient to meet Europe's needs, Congress would demand to know why more money would produce any better results.

The Marshall Plan was designed to ensure that the United States did not assume an open-ended burden but instead sponsored arrangements that would lead to future European self-sufficiency. Moreover, because the plan was supposed to cost $16.5 billion, a staggering amount of aid in 1947, the program was touted as promising to greatly expand U.S.-European trade, with a recovered Europe prosperous enough to finance purchases of American goods. This had an irresistible appeal to Congress and the country more generally. In brief, it was a plan to guard an unstable Western Europe from Communist subversion while also promoting the future prosperity of both Europe and the United States. And as Harry told Bess, "The 16.5 is for a four-year period and is for *peace*. A Russian war would cost us 400 billion and untold lives, mostly civilian. So I must do what I can."[16]

The plan worked just as designed. Although the Soviet Union and the Eastern European states would make a show of cooperation and then refuse to participate, complaining that the proposal was a device for interfering in the domestic affairs of Communist nations, the blame for the deepening European divide was then placed on Moscow. Astute commentators understood that the proposal frightened the Soviets, who believed it would allow the West to learn about Russia's weaknesses and likely encourage a more aggressive response to Soviet expansionism. Moreover, the emphasis on European self-sufficiency and U.S. benefits from revived European economies proved to be a perfect inducement to extract so much money from Congress. In the end, the plan would work so well that only $13 billion of the $16.5 billion was needed to help restore Western European living standards, which in turn undermined Communist parties and made Europe a major trading partner of the United States.[17]

At the same time, Truman also believed it essential to establish a modern national security apparatus that would prepare the United States to deal with future international conflicts. The struggle to coordinate the work of the War and Navy departments and integrate the efforts of the army and navy during World War II stood as cautionary lessons for the future. In addition, the growth in importance of airpower suggested that the United States needed a separate air arm not subordinated to either the army or the navy, although aircraft carriers would remain a vital part of the navy. Moreover, a separate intelligence service that could avert the sort of surprise attack suffered at Pearl Harbor also seemed in order, as well as some kind of agency that could coordinate diplomatic and defense policies.

The central question for a nation with antimilitary, anti-imperial traditions was how to build a national security bureaucracy without militarizing the country and setting up a secret police that spied on citizens and jeopardized its democratic freedoms. By the summer of 1947, a national consensus had emerged in support of a better prepared, more effective defense establishment. It was a response to widespread fear of another war with an aggressive Soviet Union.

The struggle to improve the country's defense organizations dogged Truman from December 1945, when he first proposed reforms, to July 1947, when Congress passed the National Security Act. The law was the result of bureaucratic battles and compromises between the military branches, the old War and Navy departments, and the White House. The act fell short of Truman's request for a defense department that unified the three armed services under a single civilian secretary. Instead, a secretary of defense oversaw a National Military Establishment with three departments administered by separate secretaries. In response to the navy, which raised the strongest objections to an integrated military, the new defense secretary was to be no more than an armed services coordinator.[18]

Only in 1949, when the ineffectiveness of

such an arrangement had become transparent, did Congress agree to Truman's insistence on a full-fledged defense secretary, who, in Truman's judgment, would have to be "the hardest, meanest son of a bitch I could find."[19] Former secretary of the navy James Forrestal had served as head of the NME until he suffered a nervous collapse in March 1949 and was replaced by Louis Johnson, a former assistant secretary of war and an influential Democratic Party fundraiser.

The 1947 legislation also established a National Security Council and a Central Intelligence Agency. To fend off the feared militarizing of the country, the heads of these agencies could be former or even serving military men, but they were not to report to any military superior. Nor was either of them supposed to preempt the activities of the FBI with investigations or policing of domestic organizations or individuals under suspicion of being spies or subversives. Lastly, neither body was invested with any policy-making authority. Their functions were to be strictly advisory and their officials were to serve at the pleasure of the president.

By the fall of 1947, Truman felt as if he were operating in a "topsy-turvy world" that was "fraught with terrible consequences" that could make the difference between war and peace. A war "just must not happen," he told Bess. "But here I am confronted with a violently opposition Congress whose committees with few exceptions are living in 1890, it is not representative of the country's thinking at all. But I've got a job and it must be done — win, lose or draw."[20]

A significant part of that "topsy-turvy world" Truman engaged with in 1947 was Middle East tensions over Zionist pressures for a Jewish homeland in Palestine. Truman entered the presidency with considerable knowledge of this dispute. As he would tell Merle Miller in an oral biography in 1961–1962, Palestine was "one part of the world that has always interested me," because of much early Bible reading. But "it wasn't just the Biblical part about Palestine that interested me. The whole history of that area of the world is just about the most complicated and most interesting of any area anywhere, and I have always made a very careful study of it," including the fact that "there has always been trouble there."[21]

In his first three years in the White House, Truman thought of the Middle East and the principal actors in the region — Arabs, British, and Jews — as nothing but trouble.

From the first, he was openly sympathetic to giving Europe's displaced Jews, who had suffered unprecedented horrors in the Holocaust, a Palestinian homeland. But sympathy did not translate readily into a means of disarming Arab hostility, helping British authorities responsible for Palestine under a League of Nations mandate, or overcoming the State Department's resistance to a policy that could arouse Arab resentment, open them to Soviet influence, and jeopardize Western oil interests. Truman also feared that pressing the Zionist case might force him "to send 500,000 soldiers there to make peace in Palestine," which, he told a press conference in 1945, he would not do. By October 1946, he was complaining that "the Jewish and Arab situation in the Near East . . . has caused us more difficulty than most any other problem in the European Theater."

Despite these difficulties, pleas to help the hundreds of thousands of displaced European Jews, whose post-Holocaust survival created a moral claim on peoples everywhere, were irresistible. A more parochial, but not trivial consideration for Truman, who was planning a presidential run in 1948, was the potential loss of Jewish support in New York, which could swing the state's large electoral vote to its governor, Thomas E. Dewey, the likely Republican candidate. Truman struggled unsuccessfully to find a solution to the Middle East dilemma. "I have about come to the conclusion," he wrote in the summer of 1946, "that there is no solution, but we will keep trying."[22]

He believed justice required an effective response to the plight of the Jews, but he resented the unrelenting pressure on the White House from Jewish Americans for help in transporting hundreds of thousands of Jewish refugees from Europe to Palestine, where they could settle in a new homeland. "Jesus Christ couldn't please them when he was here on earth, so how could anyone expect that I would have any luck?" he said at a cabinet meeting, venting his frustration. Nevertheless, the combination of humanitarian and domestic political considerations persuaded Truman, against State Department advice, to issue a public expression of support in the fall of 1946 for the partition of Palestine into Arab and Jewish states. Warned by Navy Secretary Forrestal that the United States could not afford to lose access to Arab oil, Truman responded that oil should not deter him from doing "what is right."[23]

Out of frustration with their inability to mediate Arab-Jewish differences, the British asked the United Nations to assume responsibility for a decision on the future of Palestine. When a UN committee endorsed partition as the most equitable response to Arab and Jewish demands, Truman restated his support for this solution, despite continuing opposition from the State Department's highest officials warning against loss of U.S. influence on the Arabs to the Soviets. In addition, Truman resisted State Department pressure to favor Arab control of the Negev Desert, which the UN committee was giving to Israel. Chaim Weizmann, the head of the World Zionist Organization, had convinced the president in a private meeting at the White House that Arab control of the Negev would leave it a barren wasteland whereas Jewish control would make the desert bloom.[24]

On November 29, 1947, the UN General Assembly voted in favor of the partition plan. This result elated supporters of a Jewish state and incensed Arabs. The decision provoked an outbreak of fresh violence in Palestine between Arabs and Jews, as the British announced that they would withdraw their troops from the area when partition occurred in May 1948. Discussions began at the UN regarding the need for a multi-national force to ensure against violence following partition.[25]

The moral dilemma of how to advance a just solution to the plight of Jews abroad vied with compelling pressures at home to act justly toward African Americans, who were a notoriously abused minority. The long history of discrimination and segregation, particularly in the South, was at best an embarrassing blight on an America advertising itself to the world as the defender of freedom and democracy — and at worst a gross violation of constitutional commitments to equal treatment under the law. Lynchings, systematic exclusion from the ballot box, and job discrimination had become a source of national tension that jeopardized the country's domestic tranquillity.

Because a Congress dominated by southern senators and representatives, with outsized influence over key committees — and the use of the filibuster in the Senate, where a minority could talk any legislative initiative to death — made congressional action impossible, Truman used an executive order to meet the crisis. In December 1946, he established a Committee on Civil Rights that was to suggest means of reducing, if not eliminating, racial discrimination and assuring African Americans of greater equality of opportunity in every facet of American life.

Mindful of the difficulties in making significant civil rights gains quickly, Truman was eager to give advocates of equal rights at least symbolic indications that the president stood with them. On June 30, 1947, he spoke at a National Association for the Advancement of Colored People (NAACP) rally at the Lincoln Memorial and pledged that his committee would develop a program for addressing the ills of racial discrimination. "The extension of civil rights today," he declared, "means not protection of the people *against* the government, but protection of the people *by* the government." Privately, Truman promised Walter White, the head of the NAACP, that in the future he would give substance to his remarks.

In October, Truman's committee issued an unequivocal call for equal treatment of blacks under the law in a report titled "To Secure These Rights." It urged a federal antilynching statute that would fill a void left by southern courts, which failed to convict perpetrators of mob murders of blacks. It recommended federal action to abolish poll taxes and other bars to black voting as well as integration of the U.S. armed forces and a halt to segregation on all public interstate transportation. Although Truman made no public pronouncement on the committee's report, he asked his aides to prepare a congressional message asking for action on its recommendations.[26]

Torn between competing liberal and southern factions in his party, Truman came down on the side of what he believed was both right and in the national interest. Despite warnings from Democratic Party leaders that his stand on civil rights was political suicide, Truman went ahead anyway. Politics and a reelection campaign for 1948 were not far from his mind as he ended 1947, but he lived by the proposition that what was ultimately good for the country as a whole rather than for his party or any special interest would ultimately also be to his best political advantage.

5
AGAINST ALL ODDS

Harry Truman complained constantly about the burdens of the presidency. "Liars and demagogues," in his words, abused him and he had little means to make them "behave." He told his sister in November 1947 that "all the president is, is a glorified public relations man who spends his time flattering, kissing and kicking people to get them to do what they are supposed to do anyway."[1]

He also repeatedly stated his readiness, indeed eagerness, to retire after his term was up. But the truth was that he loved political combat and relished beating opponents who had repeatedly underestimated him. He also believed — as did everyone who has ever run for the office — that he could serve the national well-being better than any of his competitors. And so he resolved to run to become president in his own name in 1948.

"The job agreed with him," says David McCullough, and Truman's close associates "were certain he would never willingly abandon it." As had been the case earlier in his political career, he loved proving that he was up "to tasks seemingly too large for him. . . . He liked being in charge. It showed in his face and in the way he carried himself."[2]

As 1948 began, the challenge was to find a winning political strategy. Whereas 1946 had been a difficult year, Truman's fortunes had improved in 1947. His appointment of George Marshall as secretary of state and his announced plans to combat Communist threats by aiding Greece and Turkey and reconstructing Europe through the Marshall Plan — combined with the stumbles of the Republican-controlled Congress — boosted his standing with the public. Opinion polls showed majority support for his foreign policies and little regard for the legislative branch. By March 1947, 60 percent of those responding to a Gallup poll endorsed the way the president was doing his job, and the number hovered there for the rest of the year.[3]

In designing a political strategy for the coming election, Truman relied on a November 1947 memorandum by Clark Clifford, his White House counsel, and James Rowe, a former White House aide to Roosevelt, which concluded that only a strong appeal to the New Deal base seemed likely to carry Truman to victory in 1948. Because the South had so consistently voted for Democratic presidential candidates since Reconstruction and because the South was so warmly supportive of the president's strong anti-Soviet actions, Clifford and Rowe believed that Truman could take the region for granted. "As always, the South can be considered safely Democratic," they wrote. "And in formulating national policy, it can be safely ignored."[4]

Instead, Clifford and Rowe focused on the threat to Truman from the left or liberals, who were, at best, lukewarm toward the president. The Left considered Truman unlikely to expand upon the New Deal reforms and were troubled by Henry Wallace's firing and by Truman's failure to sustain Roosevelt's friendly wartime relations with the Soviet Union. It was increasingly likely that the liberals would look for an alternative Democratic candidate for the presidency. And if this failed, a reduced liberal turnout at the polls could jeopardize Truman's chances in November. While liberals were not great in numbers, Clifford and Rowe asserted, they were the most articulate members of society and carried influence with millions of Americans.

The Clifford-Rowe memo also emphasized the importance of reaching out to middle-class Americans by reining in inflation and easing a housing shortage, as well as to farmers, who would shape the outcome in the West, and African Americans in northern and midwestern cities, where they could make the difference in crucial states such as New York, Illinois, Ohio, and Michigan.

The memo accurately predicted that Wallace's "Messianic belief" that "he is the indispensable man" would draw him into a third-party candidacy.[5] On December 29, 1947, Wallace announced his decision to run. The date, which was unusually early for a presidential declaration, and Wallace's lack of any party structure for a coming campaign bore out the description of him as an impractical idealist on an evangelical mission. He described his followers as a "Gideon's Army, small in number, powerful in conviction, ready for action," and predicted that "by God's grace, the people's peace will usher in the century of the common man."[6]

Although Clifford and Rowe considered

Wallace something of a crackpot, they feared that he could appeal to "gullible idealists." More specifically, Truman's challenge was to blunt Wallace's attraction to liberals by using the "bully pulpit" of the White House to announce reform initiatives that would firmly identify the president as battling the conservative Republican Congress.

The vehicle for launching the president's campaign was his State of the Union address on January 7. The president struck all the right notes with liberals and the broad middle classes: a "poor man's" tax cut; a 35-cent increase in the minimum wage (to 75 cents); federal appropriations to help expand affordable housing; increased price supports for farmers; greater spending on public education; a national health insurance program; and new conservation and public power initiatives.[7]

Truman had no illusions that the Republicans would give him any of what he asked, except for generous funding of the Marshall Plan. Nevertheless, he shared Clifford's view that his message was less a substantive design for an expanded New Deal than a call to arms in the coming election fight.

However attractive liberals might find Truman's rekindled passion for building on

Roosevelt's legacy, it was not enough to persuade them that the president was recommitted to their cause. And they too saw little likelihood that any of his proposals would be enacted.

A promise at the end of Truman's speech that he would send Congress a special message about civil rights was another matter. No issue opened a greater divide between liberals and southern Democrats than federal action on behalf of equal protection under the law for African Americans. Lynchings, denial of the ballot box, and use of state and local police authority across the South to enforce institutional racism offended most Americans. But it especially outraged liberals, who saw it as a fundamental blight on traditional American commitments to the rule of law and equality of opportunity, not to mention the embarrassment in the emerging contest with the Soviet Union for hearts and minds among peoples of color all over the world.

On February 2, Truman fulfilled his promise by asking Congress to enact comprehensive civil rights legislation. It was an unprecedented presidential request. He urged an antilynching law; expanded protection for the right to vote and elimination in particular of poll taxes that denied blacks access to the polls in seven southern states; a permanent Fair Employment Practices Commission; and an end to racial discrimination on interstate transportation facilities. He also promised to issue executive orders ending segregation in the federal government and in the armed services.

The military was a particularly glaring example of national indifference to equal opportunity and rights for African Americans. Although nearly 11 percent of enlisted men in the army were black, there was only one black colonel, who was the highest-ranking member of his race in the army. The same was true of the air force and the navy, where black officers were notable for their absence. Clark Clifford said the navy "resembled a southern plantation that had somehow escaped the Civil War. Blacks swabbed the decks, shined shoes, did the cooking, washed the dishes, and served the food. Virtually no other jobs were open to them."[8]

Truman understood that his message would receive a negative and even angry reception across the South. But he was shaken by the vehemence of the response. Southern politicians led by Governor Strom Thurmond of South Carolina told the press that the Democrats could no longer take his region for granted. In one of the more memorable printable attacks, the Mississippi House Speaker called Truman's message "damnable, communistic, unconstitutional, anti-American, anti-Southern legislation."[9] Inflammatory rhetoric filled the air waves across the South and letters poured into the White House full of invective toward the president and anyone associated with his proposals.

Truman meant what he said when he pressed the case for equality under the law. Even though he was a man with southern roots, whose ancestors had served the Confederate cause and who hailed from a part of Missouri that reflected southern mores on matters of race, he was nonetheless offended by the abuse suffered by blacks in the South. It particularly outraged him that the local authorities turned a blind eye to mob violence, including lynchings and maiming of black veterans. When a Missouri friend urged him to be cautious about provoking southern whites, Truman replied: "When the mob gangs can take four people out and shoot them in the back, and everybody in the [surrounding] country is acquainted with who did the shooting and nothing is done about it, that country is in a pretty bad fix from the law enforcement standpoint."

Yet the hostile southern response to his proposals weighed on him, and he held off sending Congress a comprehensive civil rights bill incorporating his various recommendations. Since the combination of influential southern Democrats and conservative Republicans ensured that Congress wouldn't act on the president's requests anyway, he could rationalize not sending up a bill. But his failure to take executive action during the winter and spring on desegregating the armed forces renewed liberal doubts about his commitment to their agenda.[10]

In the first six months of 1948, however, Truman had much more to think about than domestic tensions and his reelection. Communist challenges in Europe and Asia threatened America's allies and raised the specter of a possible war with the Soviet Union.

After Truman had announced the Truman Doctrine and the Marshall Plan, the Soviets saw the United States as launching an aggressive campaign to challenge their influence in Eastern, Central, and Western Europe. In response, Stalin tightened Soviet control over Poland, Hungary, and Bulgaria by purging non-Communists from their respective governments and forcing some of them to flee their countries, if they were lucky enough to escape execution or imprisonment.

Czechoslovakia and Germany were Moscow's greatest concerns. In February and March, in Prague, where there was a representative elected government, the Soviets forced non-Communist ministers from office; the pro-Western president Edvard Beneš, who was in poor health, resigned; and Jan Masaryk, the foreign minister, another friend of the West and democracy, was alleged to have committed suicide by leaping from his high-rise office. But the truth was that Soviet agents murdered him.

Moscow was especially agitated by a meeting in London from February 23 to March 6 between U.S. and Western European officials about establishing a West German state in the American, British, and French occupation zones. Nothing terrified Soviet leaders more than a revived Germany with the potential once more to become an economic and military power in Central Europe. Equally worrisome, from Moscow's perspective, was the announcement on March 17 of a fifty-year mutual defense agreement among Britain, France, Belgium, the Netherlands, and Luxembourg. Moscow saw this agreement, known as the Brussels Pact, not as a defensive pact but as an offensive alliance aimed against the Communist countries in the East.[11]

On March 17, as news of the Brussels Pact spread, the president went before a joint session of Congress to denounce the Communist destruction of Czech democracy and to emphasize America's determination to meet the Soviet challenge. He asked Congress to fully fund the Marshall Plan, enact a Universal Military Training law, and reinstate the draft. Although politics was certainly not the principal motive for the speech, his rhetoric was also calculated to raise his standing with potential voters.

It was clear to Truman and his campaign advisers that a tough anti-Communist line would be a considerable asset in the upcoming election fight. He reverted to the language of the Truman Doctrine, in which he described a struggle between worldwide communism and democracy that only a committed America could help like-minded peoples win. His evangelism was even more evident in a speech he gave that night in New York, where he reiterated his requests to Congress, depicted the United States as engaged in a battle between a godless East and a devout West — a contest between tyranny and freedom — and added a denunciation of "Henry Wallace and his Communists" for whom there was no place in the Democratic Party.

The president's speeches deepened East-West tensions, signaling the end of any hope that the two sides would trust each other — if any such possibility had ever realistically existed.[12] What each side saw as defensive actions to prevent its adversary from gaining an advantage, the other side considered acts of aggression. Such distrust is a formula for long-term conflict. And by 1948, U.S.-Soviet tensions were in full bloom.

On March 20, when the Allied Control Council for Germany met in Berlin, the meeting degenerated into an acrimonious debate over Germany's future. The Soviet military representative denounced the United States, Britain, and France for moving toward West German autonomy without regard for Moscow's interests. In response, the Soviets declared their intention to abandon council discussions as useless in sustaining East-West agreements on the German occupation. On April 1, the Soviets notified the U.S. military authority that they would subject all Americans — military and civilian — to identity checks as they moved through the 110-mile corridor (within the

Soviet occupation zone) that connected Berlin to the Western occupation zones. When the United States resisted the Soviet demands as a violation of its occupation rights and replaced road travel by a limited airlift of supplies into Berlin, the crisis quickly passed. But General Lucius Clay, the U.S. commander in Berlin, predicted that this was a foretaste of what the Allies could expect if they took steps to create a separate West German state.[13]

Tensions with the Soviet Union were not limited to Germany. In response to intelligence predicting that Moscow would pressure Norway to sign a mutual assistance agreement, which Oslo feared as a step toward being forced into the Soviet orbit, the Truman administration asked Congress to support a resolution approving U.S. participation in a regional military alliance for the North Atlantic that would become an expanded version of the Brussels Pact. With almost no debate, the Senate approved the proposal.

In June, after the Western powers issued a new single currency for the occupation zones in western Germany and then Berlin to rein in inflation, the Soviets, who saw this as a decisive step toward the creation of a West German state, announced a blockade of the Allied sectors of Berlin. All motor, rail, and river traffic from the West was barred, and electricity and food supplies from the East were also shut off to West Berlin.

The president faced a choice between ceding control of all of Berlin to Communist control, threatening military action to preserve Allied rights in the western sector of the city, or expanding the earlier airlift and relying on diplomacy to ultimately resolve the problem. Despite pressure from General Clay to act more aggressively, Truman chose to establish a daily airlift of some twenty-five hundred tons to maintain the two million residents of West Berlin for the indefinite future. Although it would take almost a year before the Soviets agreed to a resolution of the dispute, Truman was able not only to maintain the airlift but also to derive significant political and diplomatic benefits from the crisis. His resolve in the face of the Soviet threat boosted his public standing in the United States and encouraged European allies to believe that Washington would not abandon them to Moscow's bullying.[14]

The tensions with Moscow ran concurrently with difficult decisions on how to manage the crisis over Palestine. National interests, domestic politics, and moral imperatives each played a part. As the issue of a permanent partition into a Jewish and Arab state came to a head in the first months of 1948, the State Department opposed U.S. recognition of the Jewish state, emphasizing the importance of maintaining Middle East oil supplies for America's European allies. Secretary of State Marshall and his subordinates also warned that offering such recognition would permanently oblige the United States to defend the Jewish state and antagonize millions of Arabs, who might then turn to the Soviet Union for support.

Clark Clifford urged the president not to recoil from a commitment that could have serious domestic repercussions. He predicted that the Arab countries, which were so dependent on oil revenues, could not afford to shut down supplies to the West and would find little appeal in aligning themselves with the Communist superpower, which suppressed the religious practices of its own Muslim populations.

In March, as an intermediate response to these crosscurrents in the United States and the continuing violence in Palestine, Marshall, who believed he had the president's approval, directed the State Department to propose UN truce arrangements and a trusteeship that would forestall any partition. The proposals had no appeal to the contesting forces in Palestine and angered American Jews, who saw the administration as retreating from its promised support of a Jewish state and predicted Truman's defeat in the November election. The president disingenuously denied having authorized the action.

A battle now erupted at the White House between Clifford and Marshall over recognizing the nascent Jewish state, which fighting in Palestine demonstrated would now come into existence upon the British withdrawal on May 15, regardless of what the United States did.

The president sided with Clifford and decided on prompt recognition. He did not see how the United States could prevent partition, and it seemed only sensible to benefit politically from a reality it could not alter. Moreover, a Gallup poll showed 65 percent of Americans in favor of Palestine partition with only 10 percent opposed. As the historian Melvyn Leffler asserts, "U.S. officials could not dictate developments in the region. Jewish leaders would not accept trusteeship. Arab governments would not accept a truce if it envisioned Israeli independence. Why not, then, profit politically and recognize Israel? Why not, then, fulfill one's humanitarian instincts to assist the survivors of Hitler's camps?"[15] It would also prevent Moscow, which was allowing the Czechs to supply arms to the Jews in Palestine, from gaining influence in the new Jewish state without necessarily ensuring that U.S. recognition would expand Soviet influence among the Arabs.

While the establishment of Israel in May, which Truman promptly recognized, settled immediate questions about how to proceed, it left new issues unresolved: what support should Washington provide to Israel in a war for its survival with Arab neighbors and what should the United States accept as the boundaries of the new state? Inevitably, these became involved in the presidential campaign.

Beginning in the spring of 1948, everything Truman did had consequences for the election. Despite his outspoken responses to domestic and foreign problems, his public standing gave little hope that he could win in November. His appeal for civil rights reforms, the most visible of his domestic actions, had fallen flat, and had made him especially unpopular in the South. Nor did his response to the various foreign policy problems help his national standing. Polls showed him losing to three likely Republican challengers, Governor Thomas Dewey of New York, Governor Harold Stassen of Minnesota, and Senator Arthur Vandenberg of Michigan. Only the conservative senator Robert Taft of Ohio seemed unlikely to beat him.[16] When the Republican convention met in June in Philadelphia, Clare Boothe Luce, the prominent congresswoman and wife of Henry Luce, the conservative publisher of *Time* magazine, addressed the delegates. She confidently described Truman's "situation as hopeless. Frankly, he is a gone goose."[17] For the first time in sixteen years, the Republicans believed that they would restore their party's control over the White House.

Truman badly needed something to kick-start his campaign. An invitation to speak at the University of California at Berkeley became an opportunity for a cross-country precampaign tour. The idea was to travel slowly across the United States by train, which would make frequent stops and give the president an opportunity to speak to local crowds drawn by the chance to see and hear the president in person.

Truman lived, worked, and spoke from

the last car of the train, which his aides dubbed the *Ferdinand Magellan,* suggesting an exploratory adventure. The car included a rear platform with a lectern and loud-speakers and room for a handful of dignitaries to stand beside him, which made the president seem less like a remote Washington figure than an associate of each town's local officials.

The distinguishing feature of the two-week trip was thus not the six formal addresses Truman gave along the way at venues in big cities, but the informal, seemingly extemporaneous talks at the stations or "whistle stops," which was code for insignificant communities, as Senator Taft derisively called them, that struck resonant chords with thousands of people.

As Truman's biographer Alonzo Hamby described the typical scene:

> The president began a talk by alluding to some bit of local history. . . . He always introduced Bess (the "Boss") and Margaret (the "Boss's Boss"), giving the crowd a look at the womenfolk and a sense of his model middle-class family. He always displayed his customary smile and increasingly seemed to take a genuine delight in his fleeting contacts with the average

Americans who came down to the station; many of them, in turn, saw someone who might be running a local bank or small business: decent, respected, well traveled, but not much different from themselves.[18]

Observers noted how effective these informal (once, at a late-night stop in California, he appeared in bathrobe and pajamas) off-the-cuff talks were and how much people in the crowd warmed to him. "Pour it on," someone shouted at a stop in the Northwest, where the president lambasted the "worst," "do-nothing," "good-for-nothing" Republican Congress. "I'm going to — I'm going to," he shouted back.

It was estimated that three million people saw him on his two-week trip through eighteen states. When he got off the train at Union Station in Washington on June 18, *Time* described him as "full of bounce."[19]

He needed all the self-confidence he could muster. After the Republicans nominated Dewey at their convention and bolstered the ticket by making the popular California governor Earl Warren his running mate, a poll showed the president at a continuing eleven-point disadvantage in a contest with Dewey.[20] Worse, the Democrats headed into their July convention as a fragmented party.

Southern stalwarts wanted no part of Truman, and liberals, who had not already bolted to back Henry Wallace, openly advocated drafting General Dwight Eisenhower as the party's nominee.[21] Harold Ickes privately urged Truman to drop out of the running. "You have the choice of retiring voluntarily and with dignity," he told the president, "or being driven out of office by a disillusioned and indignant citizenry."[22]

Yet Truman remained confident that he would get the nomination and win the election. Few agreed with him. The Democratic delegates who came to Philadelphia, McCullough notes, "looked . . . like nothing so much as mourners at a funeral." Catching the mood of the visiting Democrats, a cabdriver declared, "We got the wrong rigs for this convention. They shoulda given us hearses." A keynote speech by the seventy-one-year-old senator Alben Barkley of Kentucky gave a spark of life to the gathering with a barn-burner address that recalled Franklin Roosevelt's twelve years of New Deal gains as a contrast with past and current Republican failings. The speech did more than ignite some enthusiasm among delegates; it won Barkley the vice presidential nomination. Truman's first choice had been the liberal Supreme Court justice William O. Douglas, but Douglas preferred to stay on the Court.

For all the intraparty doubts about Truman's candidacy, he was nominated on the first ballot, with only token opposition from southern delegates supporting Senator Richard Russell of Georgia.

The convention's most dramatic moments came with a fight over the party's platform on civil rights. Hubert Humphrey, the young and voluble mayor of Minneapolis, led an impassioned revolt against what he and his fellow liberals considered an ambiguous, restrained statement on the subject that was designed more to appease southerners than to right a historic wrong. In a floor fight demanding full-throated backing for the president's package of civil rights reforms, Humphrey and the liberals won majority support for the party, in his words, "to get out of the shadow of states' rights and walk forthrightly into the bright sunshine of human rights."

When Truman came before the exhausted delegates to accept the nomination at two in the morning on July 15, neither the late hour nor the drama of Humphrey's civil rights coup dampened his determination to turn the moment into a demonstration of his conviction that he could lead his party to victory in November. Having seen how effective his informal remarks on his recent train trip had been, he adopted the same style in a speech that lambasted the Republicans for offering empty promises and surprised the delegates and the media by announcing that he would call a special congressional session on July 26. He declared his intention to challenge the Republicans to fulfill Dewey's promises to halt inflation, ease the housing shortage, aid education, and enact civil rights reforms. It was a brilliant maneuver that threw his opponents on the defensive and gave everyone the feeling that Harry Truman had emerged as a true leader ready for a hard fight that he expected to win.

Yet Truman's fight had just begun. Two days after the Democrats ended their convention, the southerners formally bolted the party. Announcing the formation of a new political party, which became known as the "Dixiecrats," the southern Democrats nominated Strom Thurmond for president and pledged to preserve segregation. The southerners' goal was to win enough electoral votes to force the election into the House of Representatives. At the same time, Henry Wallace presided over the Progressive Party convention, which formally nominated him for president and attacked Truman's foreign policy as a prescription for another war. Despite the obvious political liability, Wallace refused to reject the support of the Communist Party of America, which, he said, shared his views on world peace.[23]

Truman's attention, however, was on the special session of Congress. The president appeared before the House of Representatives on July 26 to repeat his request for the reforms he had demanded in his convention speech. Over the next two weeks, the Congress, in defiance of the president, accomplished almost nothing, which gave Truman exactly what he wanted — a demonstration that the Republicans were unwilling or incapable of dealing with major domestic problems. In part to underscore his differences with the "do-nothing" Republicans, the president issued executive orders that fulfilled his promises to integrate the armed forces and end segregation in the federal civil service.[24]

As Truman looked forward to the fall campaign beginning in September, he found good news and bad news. The good news was that a solid majority of voters saw the Republican Congress as doing only a fair or poor job, and a slim majority believed the Democrats could do a better job of handling the nation's most important problems. The public also largely supported the president's civil rights initiatives, favoring federal jurisdiction to deal with lynching crimes and the abolition of poll taxes that impeded black voting.[25]

The bad news was that Dewey led consistently in most of the polls. Pre-September polls showed Dewey with a ten- to twelve-point advantage. Even in New York, which all observers agreed was essential for a Truman victory, the electorate favored their native son by 42 percent to 32 percent, with 14 percent backing Wallace.[26]

In October, the polls, the newspapers, the political pundits, and leaders in both parties gave Truman little chance of winning. But Truman was undeterred. He consistently hammered on the "do-nothing" Congress and the Republicans as the party of Herbert Hoover, a party that had failed to overcome the Depression and refused to accommodate itself to Roosevelt's New Deal gains that had served so many millions of current voters. And of no small consequence, Truman came across to most Americans as a man who didn't need to be president to feel good about himself. He was like most of them — plainspoken, hardworking, flawed, decent, and honest. It was a rare combination in politics, one that Dewey could not match.

Dewey was a stiff-backed character whose mustache, homburg hats, well-groomed looks, and uninspiring speaking style left people cold. The political commentator Richard Rovere described Dewey as someone who came onstage "like a man who has been mounted on casters and given a tremendous shove from behind." People made fun of him as the groom on the wedding cake or the only man who could strut sitting down. By contrast, Truman impressed one columnist as someone with "an agreeable warm heartedness and simplicity" that was "genuine."

More than personality made the difference, however. Believing he was well ahead and assured of a victory, Dewey saw little point in mounting an aggressive campaign against an opponent who was beaten anyway. Instead of launching a sustained attack against what many viewed as America's setbacks in the burgeoning cold war or blaming inflation and housing shortages on Truman's policies, Dewey spoke passively about the administration's shortcomings, fearful that beating up on someone who was so much of an underdog might do him more harm than good.

To almost everyone's amazement on Election Day, Truman defeated Dewey by more than two million popular votes, winning twenty-eight states to Dewey's sixteen and Thurmond's four, decisively beating Dewey in the Electoral College by a 303 to 189 margin. The Democrats also regained control of both houses of Congress.

Embarrassed pollsters explained their miscalculation by saying that they stopped polling too soon or failed to track shifts in voter sentiment in the last days of the campaign, when a seismic shift had occurred. But the American people, and not the pollsters, had spoken, and they rewarded Harry Truman with a four-year term not as Franklin Roosevelt's successor but as the man who deserved to be president in his own right.[27]

6
COLD WAR
PRESIDENT

However much the surprise victory elated Truman, he told reporters and a crowd of well-wishers as he left Missouri, where he had gone to vote and track the election returns, that he felt "overwhelmed with responsibility."[1] His sense of how another four years would challenge him reflected not only his understanding that second terms were almost always more difficult than first ones but also his realism about the state of the nation and the world.

Nevertheless, his victory gave him license to call upon Congress to adopt the main features of a progressive program that some described as an extension of the New Deal or the start of Franklin Roosevelt's fifth term. By contrast, Truman saw himself as setting out his own distinctive agenda that significantly went beyond anything Roosevelt had proposed. Indeed, once the war began Roosevelt had conceded that Dr. Win the War had replaced Dr. New Deal, and though he had promised a return to liberal legislative action after the war, it was more part of his fourth-term campaign than a clear program of where he would lead the nation in the postwar era.

Truman put his own special stamp on the start of his new term in January 1949 with a State of the Union message announcing that "every segment of our population and every individual has a right to expect from our Government a fair deal." Theodore Roosevelt's Square Deal and Franklin Roosevelt's New Deal now had an appropriate successor in Truman's Fair Deal.

As described in his message, the president put forth a bold agenda that would fulfill past and current hopes for a more humane and just society. He asked for a fairer, more equitable tax structure, a higher minimum wage, an expanded farm program that could raise food production and farmers' incomes, increased public power projects like the Tennessee Valley Authority, repeal of the Taft-Hartley labor law, larger social security payments, national medical insurance, federal aid to education, additional public housing programs, and the civil rights reforms that had languished in the Republican-controlled Eightieth Congress.

The last failure had left African Americans in the position of an abused minority and America open to accusations from peoples of color everywhere, who were straining to throw off white colonial rule in Africa and Asia, of being a racist society. Soviet propaganda exploited U.S. intolerance to score points in the growing competition between East and West for what was described as "hearts and minds" in the Third World.

While liberals took hope from the president's renewed call for a series of bold reforms, they and Truman quickly found that the results of the election did not translate into legislative actions. Although the Democrats had a large majority in the House, 263 to 171, and a twelve-seat advantage in the Senate, fifty-four to forty-two, it was not enough to force bills past the coalition of southern Democrats, who now held key committee chairmanships, and conservative Republicans.[2]

More was at work, however, than just conservative obstructionism. Truman's share of the popular vote in 1948 was only 49.5 percent, which meant that national sentiment was more lukewarm than enthusiastic about any bold reform initiatives. True, majorities favored increasing the minimum wage and expanded federal aid for low-rent housing, but they remained cool to labor unions, as reflected by the continuing popularity of the Taft-Hartley law. Polls showed less than majority support for national health insurance or Truman's civil rights program. The public's greatest concern was not with any of the president's proposed reforms but with the high cost of living and Communist threats to national security at home and abroad.[3]

The administration's inability to lead its Fair Deal program through Congress was made abundantly clear in March when the Senate failed to win a cloture fight against southern Democrats. Before putting any of its civil rights proposals before the Senate, the Truman administration endorsed a strategy of compelling a change in the cloture rules to allow a majority of senators present and voting to end debate rather than the current rules, which required a two-thirds majority. But with eighty-seven members present, the White House could muster only forty-one votes for its position.

"The outcome revealed the hollowness of the 1948 victory," Hamby asserts, "and plunged most liberals into deep gloom. 'It is hard to recall a more discouraging . . . legislative picture,'" James Loeb Jr., a leading member of Americans for Democratic

Action, declared. " 'Any illusion that the liberal Democrats dominate either the House or the Senate has been conclusively blasted.' "[4]

If the liberals needed any confirmation of their pessimism, it came in the congressional refusal to repeal the Taft-Hartley Act. Most of the congressmen and senators who had voted for the law in 1947 remained in office in 1949 and were not ready to see their handiwork erased. Besides, the public liked the injunctive power that Taft-Hartley gave a president to prevent a strike that could create a national emergency. Truman's efforts to drop this provision from a reform bill could not gain any traction in the House or the Senate, despite the president's assertion that the Constitution already gave him sufficient powers to deal with any potential national emergency. Taft-Hartley would remain in effect for the rest of Truman's time in the White House.[5]

What especially stood in the way of major legislative reforms was a national preoccupation with Communist aggression threatening countries friendly to the United States and the extent to which Communist subversion might be at work in Washington. The tightening Soviet domination of Eastern Europe, the ongoing crisis over Berlin (which did not end until May 1949), and a worsening situation in China, where Mao Tse-tung's Communists were making steady gains in their civil war with Chiang Kai-shek's Nationalists, aroused concerns that another world war was in the offing. And at home, the public was increasingly alarmed by allegations of Communist spies having operated inside Franklin Roosevelt's administration, including charges from Whittaker Chambers, a *Time* editor and confessed former member of the Communist Party, that Alger Hiss, a distinguished diplomat and part of the American establishment, had passed government secrets to him. It gave resonance to Republican attacks on Roosevelt's actions at the 1945 Yalta conference, where they described him as too ill to deal effectively with Stalin, who extracted commitments on Eastern Europe and Asia that critics described as tantamount to the capitulation of the European powers to Hitler at Munich in 1938. The scary conclusion was that America and the West were in danger of defeat by a Communist drive for worldwide control.

The Republican critique of Yalta had less to do with the realities faced by Roosevelt and Churchill at the time than it was a political opportunity to blame the Democrats, who controlled foreign policy, for the frustrations over postwar international developments.

Anticommunism was a transparently popular position for a politician to take in 1949. The House Committee on Un-American Activities (HUAC) was probing Communist subversion and its hearings won wide popular support, despite complaints from critics that the committee was engaged in a witch hunt that would do little or nothing to serve national security. There were calls to require loyalty oaths for labor union officers and to prevent members of the Communist Party from teaching in a college or university. Truman himself had exploited anti-Communist fears to initiate his administration's loyalty oath program and to press the administration's case for foreign aid to countries threatened by Soviet imperialism or internal Communist subversion.[6]

At the same time, however, the president had put himself on the wrong side of public sentiment when he agreed with a reporter's characterization of HUAC hearings on the Hiss-Chambers conflict as "a red herring" aimed at diverting public attention from larger domestic worries about inflation. Congressman Richard Nixon, who was building a national image as a tough-minded anti-Communist, particularly angered Truman. "All the time I've been in politics, there's only two people I hate," he said later, "and he's one."[7]

In 1949, few episodes better revealed the overblown national anxiety about a domestic Communist threat than the Senate hearings to confirm Dean Acheson as George Marshall's successor as secretary of state. There were few more acknowledged members of the American establishment than Acheson. A prominent Washington attorney, Acheson had served in Roosevelt's Treasury and State departments and then as undersecretary of state for two years during Truman's presidency, often functioning as acting secretary when James Byrnes or George Marshall was absent at international conferences.

Because Alger Hiss had also been a respected member of the American upper crust, it was conceivable to some of Truman's right-wing critics that Acheson could be a stealth Communist as well, however absurd such an accusation might be. It was Acheson, after all, who had been central in the development of the president's doctrine for aiding Greece and Turkey and the Marshall Plan. But given the current climate of suspicion in the country, even sensible members of the Senate Foreign Relations Committee felt compelled to cite an Acheson statement when confirming his appointment that declared, "Communism as a doctrine is economically fatal to a free society and to human rights and fundamental freedom. Communism as an aggressive factor in world conquest is fatal to independent governments and to free peoples."[8] But Acheson was confirmed.

The Truman administration was no less mindful of the Soviet threat than any of its Republican critics. The various actions it had taken in 1947 and 1948 to ensure Western Europe against Soviet domination culminated in the North Atlantic Treaty Organization (NATO), which the United States committed itself to in April 1949. The treaty guaranteed that if any of the other signatories were attacked, the United States would come to their aid. It was the first offensive-defensive alliance in U.S. history since the treaty with France in 1778. It put an exclamation point on the end of America's long-standing traditional isolationism and its resistance to international political commitments.

The agreement was not made without serious reservations in the State Department, among America's military chiefs, and at the White House. Since the United States already had troops stationed in Germany, it seemed superfluous for Washington to commit itself by treaty to military action against Soviet aggression. Moreover, in 1949, the U.S. military believed it lacked the resources to honor a commitment to a full-scale defense of Western Europe. The administration understood, however, that if Germany was to be rebuilt as part of a Western alliance, France needed assurances of America's future military commitment to its defense as well. French fear of German aggression was almost as pronounced as that in Moscow.

The treaty was also meant to signal the Soviets that Washington would not allow Communist domination of Western Europe by either direct aggression or subversion. But, as George Kennan warned, the alliance would militarize the cold war — the Soviets would react to NATO by establishing their own military alliance in Eastern Europe, which is exactly what happened. Moscow established a Warsaw Pact between Russia and its Eastern European satellites as a counterweight to NATO, which they depicted as a U.S. aggressive act aimed at intimidating the Soviet Union. The military buildup on both sides heightened tensions and increased the likelihood of an armed conflict.

In opposing NATO, Kennan argued that the Soviets had no intention of establishing control of Western Europe by military means. Alongside the economic and political stability the United States was supporting through the Marshall Plan, NATO was bound to provoke a pointless "military rivalry." The formal alliance would produce "a general preoccupation with military affairs, to the detriment of economic recovery and of the necessity for seeking a peaceful solution to Europe's difficulties." As Kennan also saw, such a treaty had become irresistible because, however far from reality, Western Europeans did not trust the United States to maintain its presence in the region without a formal commitment.[9]

The administration's agreement to NATO sat well with most Americans, more than two-thirds of whom approved of the pact. But the nation's confidence was shaken in September, when the Soviet Union detonated its first atomic bomb, more than five years before U.S. intelligence anticipated it would be able to do so. Where most officials, including Truman, were confident that America's monopoly on atomic bombs was its first line of defense and substantially reduced the likelihood of a Soviet surprise attack, Moscow's acquisition of the weapon changed their minds. They were fearful that the Soviets, who commanded much larger land forces in Europe and on the periphery of Asia, might now become more adventurous and even use a first atomic strike to cripple the United States and Western Europe. They also worried that their European partners might not trust U.S. determination to defend them if it meant risking a war with the Soviet Union and an atomic exchange that could devastate American cities.

Truman hesitated to announce the news of the Soviet breakthrough for fear that it would greatly upset the American and European publics. David Lilienthal, the head of the Atomic Energy Commission, tried to persuade the president to tell the public at once. Truman said he wasn't sure that U.S. intelligence had clearly demonstrated Soviet detonation of an atomic bomb, and he feared that an announcement might "cause great fears, trouble." But Lilienthal's assurances that the Soviets now had the ability to build such a weapon and that leaks about this news might undermine public confidence in the president's leadership convinced Truman to follow Lilienthal's advice. On September 23, three days after learning about the Soviet breakthrough, Truman told the world about Moscow's achievement.[10] Although there was no perceptible evidence of public distress over the Soviet advance toward military parity with the United States, it had some limited effect on Truman's own popular standing. Where the president's approval rating stood at a robust 57 percent in June 1949, it had fallen to 51 percent by the end of September.[11]

Truman now faced a critical decision. How should the United States respond to the Soviet Union's acquisition of a weapon that could eventually put it on a par with the United States and deprive America of its military deterrent to Soviet adventurism and a possible third world war? Truman gave prompt approval to a request from the Joint Chiefs to speed up the development of atomic energy. The idea was to keep ahead of the Soviets and build a larger atomic arsenal than they seemed likely to acquire in the hope that it could continue to be a meaningful restraint on Moscow.

But a much bigger decision revolved around the question of whether the president should agree to have scientists develop a hydrogen bomb, what was called the "super," a nuclear weapon that was likely to have ten times the power of the two atomic bombs used against Japan and eventually even a hundred times that capacity. Now, more than ever, the buck stopped at the president's desk.

There was sharp and even bitter disagreement over what to do. Several military and national security chiefs favored a crash program to keep America ahead of the Soviets, who were believed to be intent on developing such a powerful weapon as well. Others in the government, including George Kennan, opposed the idea as "immoral and genocidal," a weapon that could mean the end of civilization. He believed that atomic bombs and hydrogen bombs were simply not usable weapons in the hands of any sane leader. The need was for diplomacy that emphasized this point to both Soviet and American leaders, who would then find some accommodation rather than an arms race and the possibility of an apocalyptic war.

Could the United States risk holding back with the possibility that Moscow would go ahead anyway and develop a hydrogen bomb that would give it military superiority over the United States and the power to intimidate people and nations everywhere? Even if the Soviets did not intend to use such a weapon, their possession of it could be a huge psychological blow to the West. Secretary of State Acheson asked, "How can you persuade a paranoid adversary to 'disarm by example'?" He upbraided Kennan for what he called his "Quaker views" and urged him to leave the government. He told Kennan, he "had no right being in the [Foreign] Service if he was not willing to face the questions as an issue to be decided in the interests of the American people under a sense of responsibility."[12]

There the matter rested as the year came to a close.

Other international and domestic developments now became the backdrop to the president's verdict whether to develop a hydrogen bomb. Fast-moving events in Asia — Korea and China in particular — could not be ignored in Truman's calculation of what to do about U.S. military strength alongside of growing Communist power.

A joint Soviet-American occupation of Korea was one consideration in the evolving balance-of-power struggle. In September 1945, inadequate and unprepared U.S. forces landed on the Korean peninsula to liberate the Koreans from fifty years of

Japanese colonial rule. After an agreement with Moscow that Soviet forces would occupy the northern part of the country above the 38th parallel, with U.S. forces in the south, a corps under Lieutenant General John R. Hodge entered Korea without a clue as to how to manage the transition to self-rule or American governance. Hodge was so at sea that he initially left thousands of Japanese administrators in place until Korean anger forced Hodge to replace them with Koreans, who were so politically divided that the running of the country became a nightmare.

In 1948, Washington and Moscow established Korean governments in their respective zones, with the American objective to escape direct responsibility for South Korea's security as quickly as possible. Truman encouraged Syngman Rhee, the South Korean president, to use U.S. aid to build a national police force that could ensure stability inside the country and provide defense against potential external threats from the North. In 1949, with China in growing danger of becoming another Communist stronghold, Truman proposed a three-year aid program of $350 million to $385 million for South Korea, describing the country in his congressional request as a " 'testing ground' between democracy and communism, with South Korea's success held to be a 'beacon' to North Asians to resist Communism," in the words of the historian Arnold Offner. Although U.S. military chiefs considered Korea of little strategic value in the emerging Asian struggle with communism, it was an important symbol of resistance to the Soviet Union's expanded global influence.[13]

Nothing in Asia, however, was more important to an American understanding of the struggle against communism than control of China. The United States had had a long involvement with that country, mostly through religious missionaries, for over a hundred years, and there was great public sympathy for its suffering at the hands of the Japanese during World War II. Though the Nationalist government of Chiang Kai-shek was as repressive and undemocratic as, say, Mussolini's fascist Italy, many influential Americans, led by Henry Luce's *Time* magazine and encouraged by Franklin Roosevelt's White House, trumpeted China as our best hope for postwar democratic governance in East Asia.

Early in 1942, after a conference with Roosevelt in Washington, Churchill told General Archibald Wavell, the British commander of Allied forces in Asia, that he had "found the extraordinary significance of China in American minds, even at the top, strangely out of proportion. . . . If I can epitomize in one word the lesson I learned in the United States," he added, "it was 'China.' "[14]

In 1949 it was clear that Mao Tse-tung's Communists were moving toward victory over the Nationalists. At the end of April, Communist forces crossed the Yangtze River and occupied the Nationalists' capital city, Nanjing, making it now only a matter of months before they established themselves as the new rulers of the whole country. Because Stalin had been grudging in support of his Chinese comrades, out of fear that their all-out victory might bring U.S. intervention and force a confrontation with the United States and empower a rival for international Communist leadership, Mao signaled an interest in relations with the United States. First, however, Washington had to break relations with Chiang's Nationalists and agree to diplomatic and trade relations with Mao's new regime.

Although the Truman administration gave some indications that it might be receptive to ties to the revolutionary government (a direction favored by some American diplomats, missionaries, and businessmen, and calculated to serve Truman's privately stated desire to prevent a Sino-Soviet accord), the president declared himself in June unwilling to show "any softening toward the Communists." Moreover, when the U.S. ambassador in China reported the possibility that he might be welcomed in the Communist capital, Beijing, for talks, Truman vetoed the initiative and directly ordered that "under no circumstances" was the ambassador to go to Beijing.

In retrospect, it seems clear that there was no real chance of an American accommodation with the Communist regime. It did not take Mao long to see that his government's best hope for outside support and aid would have to come from Moscow, however resentful he was of Stalin's past reluctance to offer greater help. In June, Mao publicly declared that there was no third path between imperialism and socialism. In July, a Chinese mission to Moscow won promises from Stalin of a $300 million loan and military and technical assistance to combat the remaining Nationalist forces on the mainland and help China assume the role of Socialist leader throughout the East. On October 1, Mao proclaimed the People's Republic of China and declared that the

United States, with its continuing relations with the Nationalists, was the principal danger to the new regime's future security.

Whatever Truman and Acheson saw as the value of a diplomatic initiative that could impede the creation of a Sino-Soviet alliance against the West, U.S. domestic politics forestalled any real likelihood that they could act upon it. The reality of abandoning Chiang's Nationalists and agreeing to recognize Mao's Communists as China's legitimate government was certain to bring howls of protest from Chiang's influential American supporters, who would be sure to attack Truman as an appeaser all too ready to let Communists take over the world.[15]

The publication in August 1949 of *The China White Paper: United States Relations with China, with Special Reference to the Period 1944–1949* demonstrated the administration's belief that the domestic argument over China precluded any recognition of a Communist government. The appearance of this 1,054-page volume indicated not only that Truman and Acheson foresaw the end of Chiang's mainland rule but also that the Communist victory would touch off bitter recriminations over Nationalist defeat. The volume was meant to explain and justify American postwar policy in China.

Chiang's failed governance did not "stem from an inadequacy of American aid," Acheson asserted in a lengthy letter of transmittal. "Nothing the United States did or could have done within the reasonable limits of its capabilities could have changed the results." It was partly an appeal to the traditional American understanding that the United States could not fight a land war in Asia, where China's vast stretches would require an infinite number of troops and open-ended commitments of resources that the American people would never sustain.

The Nationalists' collapse, Acheson argued, was the consequence of a failed government, which could not command the loyalty of the Chinese people or field an army that had the determination to meet the severe challenges presented by Mao's more disciplined troops.

The objective of Acheson's letter and the whole volume was to win an emerging argument posed by administration critics about "how China was lost." Acheson gave the American supporters of Chiang Kai-shek — the China lobby, as it was called — a sop by declaring that the Chinese Communists were nothing more than tools of the Soviet Union. They did not represent an independent Chinese movement or speak for the

Chinese people but were subservient to Moscow and its drive for worldwide Communist control. It was an argument that Acheson did not really believe. James Chace, Acheson's biographer, asserts, "He approved this language in order to appease the China bloc and because he thought it would be little noted."

But it was a mistake. "By asserting Beijing's submissiveness to Moscow," Chace notes, Acheson "made it much more difficult to pursue a policy of recognition." Acheson may have hoped that such a characterization could encourage the Chinese people to ultimately reject Mao's rule, but it was unrealistic. By 1949, the Chinese viewed such comments as nothing more than cold war propaganda.

In the end, *The White Paper,* however persuasive it seems in retrospect, did nothing to help solve difficulties with China or to convince a majority of Americans that the administration was faultless for the debacle in China. On the contrary, it incensed the right wing, and the China lobby used it as a launching pad for an unrelenting attack on the administration as weak on fighting communism in China and in Asia generally. The China lobby also branded Truman, Acheson, and the whole State

Department as an utter failure in protecting the United States from the rising tide of international communism.

Chace quotes administration critics, who called *The White Paper* "a smooth alibi for the pro-Communists in the State Department who had engineered the overthrow of our ally the Nationalist Government of the Republic of China" and described the volume as "a 1,054-page whitewash of a wishful, do-nothing policy which has succeeded only in placing Asia in danger of Soviet conquest."

When Chiang withdrew from the mainland in December 1949 and joined some 300,000 Nationalist troops, who had managed to escape to the offshore island of Formosa (also known as Taiwan), a new controversy erupted over how the United States should respond to Chiang's appeal to help him defend the island against a Communist invasion and create a base from which he could eventually launch a return to the mainland. Truman and Acheson accepted the advice of the Joint Chiefs that Formosa was not crucial to American security in East Asia and did not warrant military intervention to protect Chiang's forces there or aid them to launch an eventual invasion of the mainland with the unlikely prospect of

176

overthrowing Mao's Communists.

The decision brought further attacks on the administration for being too passive toward communism's victory in China. Truman and Acheson expected Mao to seize Formosa in 1950, which would then eliminate the Nationalists as an element in the debate over China and open the way to an American policy of eventual recognition that could split the emerging Sino-Soviet coalition. But when no invasion occurred, it left Chiang as a continuing presence in the U.S. domestic dispute over China policy and froze the United States into a position of long-term antagonism to Communist China, which the Chinese were only too happy to reciprocate.[16]

Looking back almost sixty years later, it is astonishing that so unrealistic or irrational a critique of administration policy on Nationalist collapse could get so receptive a hearing in a nation that prided itself on reasoned public discourse in support of wise national decision making. Although 64 percent of the country had heard or read nothing about *The White Paper*, the 34 percent who had were critical of its arguments. Fifty-three percent of these attentive Americans thought that the administration had "blundered" badly in its handling of the Chinese civil war by failing to give the Nationalists more help, though no one could say just how this help might have made a difference. In November, 76 percent of a survey said that they had heard about China's civil war and only 20 percent of these Americans wanted to recognize the new regime; 42 percent were opposed.[17]

The country seems to have been terrified by the sudden postwar turnabout from an America that had defeated the forces of totalitarianism everywhere in 1945 to a nation that seemed vulnerable now both at home and abroad to a new totalitarian threat with an apparent military capacity comparable to America's. Moreover, Americans faced the frightening realization that the Communists were winning the argument against the United States with hundreds of millions of people everywhere: communism seemed to offer them more hope than a materialistic and "soulless" society that was more committed to self-indulgence than to any ideology that promised poor folks happier times ahead.

The public reaction to events in China was a perfect demonstration of Albert Einstein's observation that everyone who hoped for public reason and justice needed to be "keenly aware [of] how small an influence reason and honest good will exert upon events in the political field."

What made the fight over China even more difficult for Truman was that it occurred in the context of allegations that he presided over an administration that was corrupted by cronyism. In particular, General Harry Vaughn, the president's military aide and his friend dating from their service in World War I, was accused of facilitating government contracts for friends and arranging for Bess Truman to receive a scarce freezer for the Truman home in Independence in 1945. Critics now characterized the administration not only as being manipulated by Communists like Alger Hiss but also as being in the pockets of sleazy businessmen, who received favored treatment from Vaughn.

Despite the unflattering public picture, Truman, who was intensely loyal to old friends and knew that Vaughn had done nothing illegal, refused to dismiss him. As Robert Donovan explained, Vaughn was an amusing companion with a sharp wit and an affinity for barnyard stories that lightened Truman's days. He "made Truman laugh when he needed to — a service not without its value to the state." Asked by a reporter whether the president intended to remove

Vaughn for his indiscretions, Truman snapped, "He will not." Truman paid a "rather steep price" for "such *divertissement*," in Donovan's words.[18]

Ronald Reagan's secretary of state George Shultz said that in politics trust is the coin of the realm, and once a president and the people around him lose credibility with the press and the public, it makes it nearly impossible to provide effective leadership. A leader who is seen as untrustworthy cannot lead. At the very least, it opens him to attacks that further erode confidence in his judgment and the acceptance of what he proposes as necessary for the national well-being. The doubts that surfaced about Truman in 1949 would cast a shadow over his remaining three years in office and make every decision a test of whether he was acting wisely in the national interest.

7
MISERIES AT HOME AND ABROAD

On January 4, 1950, the president went before a joint session of Congress to report on the State of the Union. Deference toward the office of the president traditionally dictated a degree of decorum that mutes the partisan politics that invariably exists between the opposing party and the occupant of the White House.

Truman's appearance in 1950 was different. After the unexpected and bitter defeat in 1948 and seventeen years of Democratic presidents, with three more years to go, the Republicans could not contain their anger at an administration they now saw as jeopardizing the nation's security. Truman's critics were enraged by the Soviet Union's control of Eastern Europe, its acquisition of the atomic bomb, and the loss of China to communism, and they saw Truman as wretchedly shortsighted in meeting Communist dangers at home and abroad. Although the Republicans had no better ideas on how to answer these threats, politics dictated that they decry the president's performance as falling short of what they could accomplish in his place.

When the president characterized the state of the nation as "good" and dangers in Europe and the Mediterranean as having receded, the opposition sat silent as Democrats applauded. When the president complained that the Republican tax cuts in the previous Congress had left the country with insufficient revenue to meet its domestic and foreign obligations, however, his statement provoked boos, jeers, and dismissive laughter. Truman paused, smiled, and turned beet red with anger as he carried through to the end of his speech.[1]

It was the first of a renewed series of attacks on Truman during the remainder of his term. The first blow came on January 22, when a jury convicted Alger Hiss of perjury, for lying under oath about passing government documents to Whittaker Chambers. Dean Acheson's public refusal to turn his back on Hiss gave a semblance of truth to accusations that the administration was shielding its Communist officials, who were weakening its determination to stand up for U.S. global interests. Richard Nixon accused the Truman White House of a "deliberate" attempt to hide the truth about Hiss and other Communist conspirators in the administration. Senator Joseph McCarthy of Wisconsin wanted to know if Acheson's statement about Hiss meant that he would "not turn his back on any other Communists in the state department." Hugh Butler, the junior Republican senator from Nebraska, decried Acheson's "smart-aleck manner and his British clothes and that New Dealism in everything he says and does, and I want to shout, 'Get out! Get out! You stand for everything that has been wrong in the United States for years.' "[2]

A second blow came on February 4, when British authorities arrested the physicist Klaus Fuchs, who had worked in the Manhattan Project, for having passed secrets to Soviet spies, another news report that added to the belief that the Democrats had been complicit or lax in protecting the country from Communist espionage.[3]

The Hiss and Fuchs cases were immediate backdrops to the president's decision to move forward on building a hydrogen bomb. No president can entirely resist domestic crosscurrents about foreign dangers, and this was certainly true of Truman's decision to build the "super" bomb. But Truman also had genuine fears of a Soviet advantage that exceeded any worries about political re- criminations. At the same time, as he gave the go-ahead to develop the hydrogen bomb, Truman commissioned a study of America's defense needs to protect itself from alleged Soviet plans for worldwide conquest. The report, which was given the designation NSC-68, would be completed in April. It began with the assumption that the Soviets were driven by "a new fanatic faith antithetical to our own" that aimed at establishing "absolute authority over the rest of the world."[4]

The objective in NSC-68 was to put forward a strategy not just to contain the Soviets in the hope that their system would eventually wither and die, but to defeat the Communists in an intensely competitive cold war. Under this plan, annual defense spending was to grow from $14.3 billion to $50 billion, a fourfold increase from 5 percent to 20 percent of gross national product. The report did not rule out nego- tiations with Moscow, but any talks were to be done from a position of clear military superiority, which would force the Soviets into concessions or to back away from their plans for worldwide conquest.[5]

The report, Dean Acheson said later, was

meant to create conditions that could intimidate Moscow. But it also aimed "to so bludgeon the mass mind of 'top government' that not only could the President make a decision but that the decision could be carried out," meaning that resistance in the government to such huge increases in defense spending from fiscal conservatives would be overcome.[6] On this point, Truman had public support: 40 percent of Americans saw war as the nation's greatest problem, and 63 percent favored larger military outlays.[7]

But the public was responding less to the administration's objective assessments of Soviet intentions and more to the fears generated by Truman's domestic political critics, notably Senator Joseph McCarthy of Wisconsin. McCarthy spoke with a convincing passion about the Communist danger at home that resonated with millions of Americans. In February 1950, in a speech before the Republican Women's Club in Wheeling, West Virginia, he charged that 205 Communist spies worked in the State Department. When McCarthy followed his speech with a telegram to the White House, he stated that he had in his possession "the names of 57 communists who are in the State Department at present." A week later

185

in remarks on the Senate floor the number had risen to eighty-one. Because the press gave extensive coverage to McCarthy's allegations, it became impossible for the Senate to resist hearings on the charges.[8]

And because McCarthy was so evasive about what he had as solid evidence about the Communist danger, he can be seen as a political opportunist who saw an issue ripe for public consumption and used it to gain political advantage for himself and his party. Truman dismissed McCarthy then and later as a charlatan, "a ballyhoo artist who has to cover up his shortcomings by wild charges." The president also privately described him as a "pathological liar" and characterized his attacks as part of the 1950 congressional election campaign.[9]

Truman also attributed McCarthy's overnight appeal to a recurring national affinity for hysteria about an apocalyptic danger like the Red Scare of 1919–1920. Frightened by the Bolshevik revolution in Russia, which was promising to topple established authority around the world, and by the presence of anarchists in the United States, some of whom exploded a bomb on Wall Street, American business and political leaders supported the suspension of civil liberties and the expulsion of radical aliens from the country. Similar fears surfaced in the late 1940s and early 1950s.

Truman considered McCarthy to be Stalin's best ally in undermining a bipartisan foreign policy that could effectively meet the Soviet threat. After McCarthy destroyed himself in 1954, when his ruthless abuse of the truth came to light during the televised army-McCarthy congressional hearings, Truman felt fully vindicated by his understanding of what a vicious and unconstructive public figure McCarthy was.

But no one could deny that during his years of influence between 1950 and 1954, he effectively poisoned the public's mind with unsubstantiated charges against men and women who, whatever their politics, were no significant threat to the republic's survival. He was an ingenious demagogue who made the rise of a national security state impossible to resist. To be sure, even without McCarthy, the Truman administration would have felt compelled to meet the Soviet threat with hydrogen bombs and the fulfillment of the preparedness program outlined in NSC-68. But the exaggerated fears that McCarthy spawned made America a less open, less democratic society, with public receptivity to political charges of unpatriotic weakness by one party against another for failing to be sufficiently steadfast in meeting external and internal dangers. A conviction that political gains can be made by exaggerated attacks on an opponent's insufficient militancy about the country's real and alleged enemies has become an ugly mainstay of America's perpetual political campaigns.

The Communist threat, abetted by McCarthy's exaggerated charges, produced a dramatic shift in America's traditional relations with the nations of East Asia. With a belief after 1948 that the Soviet threat in Europe and the Mediterranean was being contained, national anxieties about communism focused on the far side of the Pacific. China, once America's benign friend, which had been victimized by Western and Japanese imperialism, suddenly became America's archenemy: a Communist power intent on spreading its antidemocratic poison across East Asia. Japan, by contrast, America's traditional rival for influence and markets in the region, became our best hope for creating a model democratic, prosperous capitalist society.

Southeast Asia and Korea, which had been peripheral areas of U.S. concern before 1945, had become regions of greater concern in the postwar world. True, the United

States was eager for the British, Dutch, and French to resume their traditional responsibilities for their Southeast Asian colonies, though with more liberal policies aimed at ultimate self-determination. But the Asians' justifiable distrust of European intentions turned into rebellions, which drove the Truman administration into a new preoccupation with Asian affairs.[10]

Nowhere was this more true than in Korea. From the start of the U.S. occupation in 1945, the Truman administration had been working to limit its involvement with Korea by encouraging Seoul's autonomy and United Nations responsibility for the country's future. The U.S. military withdrew from the peninsula in 1948 and 1949, and in private discussions and public statements Washington made clear that it did not see Korea as vital to U.S. strategic needs in a worldwide or Asian war.

Unknown to the president or any American policymakers, North Korea's president, Kim Il Sung, had lobbied Stalin in March, August, and September 1949 and again in January 1950 to let him launch an attack against the South. Stalin's initial reluctance gave way to approval in 1950. As Don Oberdorfer, a leading expert on Korea, concluded in a 1997 book, "Scholars are still unsure what led to Stalin's reversal." Oberdorfer speculates that it could have been the withdrawal of U.S. forces and a famous Dean Acheson statement excluding Korea from a U.S.-Asian defense perimeter, the Soviet atomic bomb, or Mao's victory in China.[11]

On June 25, 1950, North Korean forces crossed the 38th parallel, with Kim denouncing Rhee's unpopular government in the South as a U.S. colonial surrogate. Kim promised to unify Korea and to ensure its self-determination with democratic elections — a promise no observer of Communist practices could take seriously.

Truman faced several difficult choices: Should he stick to strategic assumptions about the limited importance of Korea to American national security and allow the North to win what seemed like a sure victory; or should he intervene by rushing in U.S. forces, stationed in Japan, to halt and eventually defeat the North's attack? And if he decided on a military response, could he simply invoke his powers as commander in chief or did he need to ask Congress for a declaration of war? What role should he ask the United Nations, which had taken responsibility for Korea since 1948, to play?

The answers were not long in coming.

Truman concluded, for both international and domestic considerations, that he needed to meet the North Korean aggression head-on. His principal analogy was the Munich appeasement of Hitler's aggression against Czechoslovakia in 1938. If he allowed the North Koreans to overwhelm a U.S. ally, would it not embolden the Soviets, who might feel freer to reach for greater control in Europe and the Mediterranean? And might it not give the Chinese hope of expanding their influence and control into Southeast Asia? Would it not also embolden the Japanese Communist Party? "Korea is the Greece of the Far East," Truman told an aide on June 26. "If we just stand by, they'll move into Iran and they'll take over the whole Middle East. There's no telling what they'll do if we don't put up a fight now."

Although he had next to nothing to say about the domestic pressures on him to respond to the attack, they were part of his calculations as well. Allowing South Korea to fall would have intensified the right-wing attack on his administration as a collaborator with the Communists, who were exploiting the weakness of an irresolute president. Moreover, understanding how essential it was to move quickly, Truman did not hesitate to direct U.S. forces to join the fight and to call on the United Nations to stand up to an act of overt aggression that challenged the very principles of that organization.

As it turned out, the Soviets were boycotting the UN Security Council, in protest of the world body's refusal to recognize the People's Republic of China as the legitimate government of that country. With the Communist superpower absent, the UN immediately condemned the attack. The Soviet absence may have been a signal that Beijing (and not Moscow) had been the principal backer of Kim's decision to invade, or at least Moscow may have wanted it to appear that way. While the Soviets would not join any condemnation of the aggression, they may also have been insulating themselves from any American impulse to turn the conflict into a wider war with the Soviet Union.

To blunt any suggestion that he had bypassed the Congress and the Constitution in ordering military action, Truman declared that the United States "was working entirely for the United Nations." The president told the press that he was collaborating with the UN "to suppress a bandit raid." When a reporter asked if

Truman believed he was engaged in a "police action," he replied, "Yes. That is exactly what it amounts to." This decision left him free to fight the war without feeling the need to ask for a congressional resolution, which was certain to pass, but would have given right-wing opponents an opportunity to repeat their complaints about the president's handling of China and the growth of Communist influence in Asia.[12]

The initial fighting gave the North a distinct advantage. U.S. military planners and State Department officials had assumed that Rhee's forces could hold their own and perhaps even beat back any attack from the North. But to their surprise, the North Koreans routed their southern counterparts. They quickly captured Seoul and seemed poised to take control of the entire peninsula. When General Douglas MacArthur, the commander of all U.S. forces in Asia, visited the battlefront on June 29, he predicted that the North would win a quick victory unless he was allowed to deploy U.S. ground troops stationed in Japan to Korea. Truman agreed, and on June 30, a regimental combat team was sent to Korea with additional forces to follow as quickly as possible.

Truman and Acheson saw the battle for

Korea as essential to stem further Communist advances around the globe. By fighting in Korea, the administration hoped to demonstrate to Stalin and Mao that America was prepared to contest aggression wherever it occurred — even in as secondary a theater as Korea.

Within a matter of weeks, American air, sea, and ground forces halted and began reversing the North's success. On September 18, in a brilliant, unexpected amphibious landing at Inchon, behind North Korean lines, MacArthur's forces caught the North Koreans in a pincer and drove them back up the peninsula. On September 29, MacArthur recaptured Seoul and by the beginning of October, the South had been liberated from Kim's troops.[13]

The great issue now facing the president was whether to cross the 38th parallel, complete the defeat of Kim's forces, and free North Korea from Communist rule. As early as September 11, Truman had issued an order authorizing MacArthur to prepare to cross the parallel. Truman's reasoning rested on the conviction that the restrained Soviet and Chinese response to America's defeat of the North Korean troops signaled their reluctance to intervene in the fighting. During September, the Soviet UN delegation discussed "a cease-fire, internationally supervised elections, and a unified Korea." Washington policymakers thought that current developments provided "the United States and the free world with a first opportunity to regain territory from the Soviet bloc. . . . Throughout Asia, those who foresee only inevitable Soviet conquest would take hope."[14]

Domestic political considerations were not absent from Truman's thinking. Congressional elections were only a month off, and a failure to seize the opportunity to destroy a Communist regime that had committed an act of such overt aggression would be a political gift to the Republicans, who were only too happy to continue their political assault on Truman and the Democrats as soft-minded liberals all too ready to appease Communists at home and abroad. Moreover, 64 percent of a Gallup poll wanted the United States to continue fighting after pushing North Korean forces above the parallel and to force North Korea to surrender.[15]

While Truman was inclined to cross the parallel, he also wished to proceed cautiously. MacArthur was told to stop American troops from entering North Korea if Soviet or Chinese forces appeared in the

North. Moreover, even if U.S. units crossed the parallel, they were not to accompany the South Koreans to the border areas with China or Russia. With the Chinese issuing repeated warnings through their press and foreign embassies that an invasion of North Korea would provoke their intervention, Truman decided to meet General MacArthur in the Pacific on Wake Island on October 14.

His motives for traveling seventy-five hundred miles from Washington and bringing his commanding general so far from the war zone were, Alonzo Hamby explains, "highly mixed." He wanted to meet MacArthur face-to-face for the first time, get his direct assessment of the consequences of a move into North Korea, and "perhaps most important, secure a good photo opportunity with an American hero against a backdrop of unfolding victory. The upcoming midterm elections — crucial to the future of Truman's Fair Deal — were less than a month away. It appears certain that worry about Chinese intervention was not uppermost in the president's mind."[16]

Because Truman had crossed swords with MacArthur both before and after the Wake Island meeting, the president later gave a distorted account of their encounter. In

August, after MacArthur had visited Chiang Kai-shek on Formosa and issued a public blast at the Truman administration for failing to forcefully endorse Chiang's Formosa enclave as a counter to Asian communism, Truman compelled him to withdraw his statement.

Later events would add to the Truman-MacArthur differences, and Truman told Merle Miller in a conversation for his 1972 book that MacArthur was "a dumb son of a bitch." During their conference at Wake Island, Truman said, MacArthur was arrogant in public, but "kissed my ass at that meeting." The get-together, however, was anything but abrasive. Truman's complaints — that MacArthur had been rude to his commander in chief by arriving late in sloppy dress to greet the president as he descended from his plane, for which Truman claimed he reprimanded him — were not true. Nor was Truman skeptical of MacArthur's assurances of quick success; "the war will be over by Thanksgiving and I'll have the troops back in Tokyo by Christmas," Truman quoted MacArthur to Miller, to show how wrong the general was.[17]

The meeting, in fact, was entirely cordial. In a half-hour private conversation, the general assured the president that victory was in sight in Korea, that the Chinese would not intervene, and that he'd be able to transfer a division of troops to Europe by January 1951. At a larger meeting lasting two hours with military and White House staffs, MacArthur described the chances of a Chinese intervention as "very little." As for the Russians, he said they lacked the military wherewithal to help the Chinese if they did intervene, and he predicted that the Chinese would suffer "the greatest slaughter."

Subsequent communiqués and statements about the meeting were all sweetness and light, describing their complete accord on current success and future plans. Once U.S. forces crossed the 38th parallel, however, MacArthur disregarded orders to keep American troops away from the northern border areas, explaining to the Joint Chiefs that such deployments were essential for success. No reprimand arrived from the Pentagon or the White House. There seemed no reason to argue with MacArthur's apparent success. Besides, it was difficult to challenge his authority after the victory at Inchon.

By the last week of October, however, reports indicated that Chinese troops had crossed into North Korea from Manchuria, and by the first week of November, U.S. intelligence was estimating that possibly forty thousand Chinese soldiers had entered the fighting. On November 5, MacArthur told the press that the Chinese army had joined the conflict and more troops were massing in Manchuria. Privately, MacArthur asked permission to bomb the bridges over the Yalu River (the boundary separating Manchuria and North Korea) to stem the movement of Chinese forces. Fearful that he was now facing a new, wider war, Truman saw no option but to grant MacArthur's request. But he did not want any U.S. air attacks on the Chinese in Manchuria lest it provoke the larger conflict Truman still hoped to avoid.

As conditions deteriorated in Korea, other distressing events occurred at home. Two Puerto Rican nationalists traveled to Washington from New York with the intent of assassinating the president. They wished to call the world's attention to a demand for Puerto Rico's independence from U.S. control, which had existed since the Spanish-American War in 1898. Unlike Cuba, which had regained its independence, Puerto Rico remained a semiautonomous part of the United States. Ironically, Truman had publicly supported Puerto Rico's right to determine its relationship with the United States by a majority vote of its citizens. The assassins represented a small element on the island that wanted an immediate grant of nationhood.

On November 1, the two men attacked the policemen guarding the president at Blair House, where the first family was living while the White House living quarters were being renovated. They managed to kill one guard and wounded two others, but one of the would-be assassins was killed and the other captured before they could break into the house and shoot Truman, who was taking an afternoon nap in an upstairs bedroom. Although the captured assailant would be convicted of murder and sentenced to execution in 1952, Truman would commute his sentence to life imprisonment. (President Jimmy Carter would pardon him in 1981.)

Truman confided to his diary after the terrible incident, "It's hell to be President," and he described himself in a letter to a friend as "really a prisoner now." Morning walks, which had been a pleasant recreation for him, were now less available and more closely guarded; the Secret Service insisted that even the short walk across the street from Blair House to the Oval Office be made in a bulletproof car.

David McCullough concludes his compelling description of this traumatic episode with the observation that Truman "had always imagined he might take care of any would-be assassin, as had Andrew Jackson, who, when shot at by a deranged assailant at the Capitol, went after the man with his cane."[18]

On November 7, the country went to the polls to elect a new Congress. Circumstances favored the Republicans. In addition to the usual shift away from the governing party in a midterm election, Truman and the Democrats were burdened by tax increases forced by war costs and fears of shortages and inflation, as the country had experienced in World War II. The apparent involvement of China in the Korean fighting by November 7 amplified worries that the conflict would turn into a third world war. In August, well before any evidence of Chinese participation in the fighting, 57 percent of Americans thought the United States was already in World War III.

The elections also featured a vicious attack on the president and the Democrats as having encouraged the North Korean aggression by weak responses to the Soviets and Chinese Communists. Joe McCarthy said that "the Korean death trap, we can lay at the doors of the Kremlin and those who sabotaged rearming, including Acheson and the President, if you please." McCarthy took special aim at Senator Millard Tydings of Maryland, who had vigorously opposed his distorted charges against the administration about Communist appeasement. McCarthy encouraged his allies in Maryland to publicize doctored photos of Tydings in conversation with the U.S. Communist Party leader Earl Browder.[19]

Tydings lost and so did another prominent liberal Democratic senator, Helen Gahagan Douglas of California, who fell victim to Richard Nixon's attacks on her as a fellow traveler of Communists; his campaign distributed flyers labeling her the "Pink Lady." It wasn't simply that the Republicans won 52 percent of the vote to the Democrats' 42 percent and that Democrats lost five seats in the Senate, cutting their advantage to two votes, and twenty-eight seats in the House, where their lead was reduced to twelve. It was the belief that McCarthy and the anti-Communist drumbeaters were now in political control of the country. As the liberal historian Arthur Schlesinger Jr. told Averell Harriman, "I do not see how the elections can be honestly interpreted except as a triumph for McCarthyism."[20]

The election losses frustrated and angered Truman. It was one thing for voters to turn against him and the administration for economic or foreign policy failures. But to see folks taken in by McCarthy's anti-Communist antics was infuriating. The evening of the elections he took refuge on the presidential yacht in Chesapeake Bay, where, in a rare display of lost self-control, he drank himself into a stupor. Before the press, however, he refused to acknowledge that he was greatly disturbed by the election results.[21] Besides, for the moment, the war in Korea remained a success that gave him hope of quieting the right-wing outcry.

But by late November the situation in Korea had turned into a disaster. After the initial thrust into North Korea at the beginning of November, the Chinese seemed to retreat back across the Yalu River. As a consequence, MacArthur prepared a "final offensive," which he launched on November 24 without a full endorsement from the Joint Chiefs in Washington. MacArthur divided his forces in two, sending troops up the east and west sides of the Korean peninsula. The Chiefs believed it a risky strategy and had also warned against proceeding to the Yalu.

MacArthur shunned their caution and four days later found his troops under siege from Chinese forces measuring between 250,000 and 300,000 men. MacArthur cabled the Chiefs that the United States now faced "an entirely new war." He demanded reinforcements, asked permission to call in Chinese Nationalist forces from Taiwan, bomb Chinese bases in Manchuria, and chase Chinese combat planes across the Yalu. Truman and his top advisers were alarmed and now feared that any further escalation could provoke a wider war with China and possibly the Soviet Union. When the White House rejected his requests, MacArthur told the press that he was operating under "an enormous handicap, without precedent in history."[22]

During a November 28 cabinet meeting that included military advisers, Truman and Acheson emphasized their determination to hold the line in Korea at the same time as they tried to avert a larger war. But at a press conference two days later, which Truman held to reassure the public that he was strong in his determination, the president unnerved Americans and European and Asian allies by responding affirmatively to a reporter's question about considering the use of using atomic bombs. He then added to the anxiety by denying any need for UN authorization and declaring that "the military commander in the field will have charge of the use of the weapons."

The president's remarks frightened European allies, who pressed Truman through British prime minister Clement Attlee to consider negotiating a cease-fire with the Chinese and withdrawing from Korea to ensure against a larger war and not to give the Soviets a justification for aggression in Europe. During White House meetings with Attlee in the first week of December, Truman and Acheson were adamant about not abandoning Korea. They argued that a U.S. withdrawal would lead to the loss of not only Korea but all of Southeast Asia to communism. They described China as nothing more than a Soviet surrogate intent not on national self-preservation but Communist control everywhere. The president assured Attlee that he alone could authorize use of atomic bombs, and that he had no current intention of doing so. He also promised to consult the British before ever taking such action. Truman and Acheson also emphasized their determination to avoid a wider war, but explained that the current political mood in America left them no choice but to continue fighting in Korea.[23]

If the stressful developments in Korea weren't enough to overwhelm Truman, on December 5 his old friend and press secretary Charlie Ross suddenly died of a heart attack. At the age of sixty-five, Ross was a year younger than the president. Truman was so distraught he could not read a statement to the press about his sense of loss. The measure of his distress, however, registered more clearly the following day when he wrote a scathing letter to the *Washington Post* music critic, who had published a harsh commentary on a concert vocal performance by Truman's daughter, Margaret. Truman's letter found its way into the press. In a later graphic description to Merle Miller of what he had written, he said, "If I could get my hands on him I'd bust him in the jaw and kick his nuts out."[24]

The Korean developments and Truman's intemperate letter drove his public standing to an all-time low. The *Chicago Tribune* wondered whether the president's "mental competence and emotional stability" were sufficient for him to remain as president. One letter writer told the president that his "concern" with his daughter's career was "ridiculous" at a time when the country was in such danger from foreign threats.[25] Truman rationalized his letter by saying it was the sort of thing any father would do, but, of course, he wasn't any father. His outburst was an inexcusable personal and political display of emotionalism that the public never wants to see from a president.

On December 15, Truman felt compelled to announce a national emergency. He declared the country in "great danger." He forecast controls and rationing reminiscent of World War II. He also announced the creation of an Office of Defense Mobilization. Behind the scenes, the crisis spurred Truman to prepare for a third world war. He asked Congress for supplemental defense appropriations to expand the army, navy, and air force and dramatically increase armaments, including the country's atomic arsenal. But the consensus every president needs to sacrifice blood and treasure in a war had disappeared.[26]

8
LOST CREDIBILITY

With two years remaining in his presidency, Truman badly needed to reestablish his credibility with the public over his management of foreign affairs if he was to effectively meet the national security challenges that lay ahead.

At the start of 1951, however, large majorities did not trust his judgment on Korea, where he remained determined to save the country from a Communist takeover. Sixty-six percent of a survey said they favored a withdrawal of U.S. forces from the fighting as fast as possible; only 25 percent wanted to continue the conflict against the Chinese.

More bad news from Korea at the end of December and early January added to Truman's problems with holding public support for a sustained war effort. The death of the U.S. commanding general in Korea, Walton Walker, in a jeep accident in late December coupled with the retreat of

U.S. forces in January below the 38th parallel and the loss of Seoul deepened American pessimism about the fighting. And although U.S. resistance under General Matthew Ridgway, Walker's replacement, stiffened in late January, when he halted the Chinese advance some fifty miles south of Seoul, it did little for Truman's public standing. Neither did Ridgway's counteroffensive, which drove the Chinese out of the South Korean capital by the middle of March. Just 21 percent of the country thought the president should run for another term, and at the end of March his approval rating remained at a depressing 28 percent.[1]

Worse developments were in the offing. By late March, the Truman administration had made clear that it had no intention of marching north again across the parallel or carrying the war into China itself. It was receptive to a cease-fire that could restore the prewar lines and regimes in control of South and North Korea. These announcements did not sit well with General MacArthur, who considered Truman's position to be a betrayal of his effort in Korea and an appeasement of China that would leave the Far East in perpetual danger from Communist expansion. MacArthur issued a statement on March 24 that was calculated to short-circuit the president's efforts to negotiate a cease-fire. MacArthur announced that the successful U.S. offensive demonstrated China's incapacity to defeat UN forces in Korea, and publicly urged the Chinese to enter into surrender talks or face the prospect of a wider war in which their military might and their domestic political control would be destroyed.

MacArthur's statement successfully forestalled negotiations. The Chinese, who did not see themselves as defeated in Korea, would not submit to humiliating peace talks dictated by MacArthur. The general's public pronouncement increased the prospect of a military stalemate, which he and his Republican congressional allies assumed would eventually compel the administration to take "strong retaliatory measures" that would result in the wider war with China that MacArthur believed essential to America's long-term national security. Although Truman considered dismissing MacArthur for defiantly announcing a policy at variance with White House intentions, he hesitated to take on the general, who, despite considerable recent criticism in the press for his overly optimistic assumptions about the outcome of crossing the 38th parallel, remained an untouchable national icon.[2]

MacArthur, however, passed the bounds of permissible defiance of presidential authority on April 5, when the House minority leader, Joseph Martin, released to the press a letter that MacArthur had written to him. In the letter, MacArthur expressed support for Congressman Martin's idea of unleashing Chiang Kai-shek's Nationalist troops to invade mainland China and open a second front in the Korean War. MacArthur also predicted that unless the war in Korea was expanded to China, the United States would ultimately lose the struggle for control of Asia, which in turn would mean the loss of Europe to the Soviets and American defeat in the worldwide conflict with the Communists.

MacArthur declared that it was "here in Asia . . . where the Communist conspirators have elected to make their play for global conquest. . . . If we lose the war to Communism in Asia the fall of Europe is inevitable, win it and Europe most probably would avoid war and yet preserve freedom." MacArthur concluded his letter by saying, "There is no substitute for victory."

There have been few less accurate assessments of what needed to be done to ensure long-term U.S. and European national security. MacArthur's recommendations are in a league with later misjudgments by President Lyndon B. Johnson, who thought that U.S. air and ground forces could preserve Vietnam's autonomy; by President Richard Nixon, who believed that Vietnamization or the training and equipping of South Vietnam's military could save it from a North Vietnamese takeover; and by President George W. Bush, who mistakenly assumed that U.S. arms could replace Saddam Hussein's totalitarian rule in Iraq with an American-style democracy. MacArthur's recommendations were a demonstration of how wrong "the best and the brightest" can sometimes be.

On April 10, after consultation with the Joint Chiefs, the cabinet, and Democratic congressional leaders, Truman informed MacArthur that he was relieved of all his commands and must retire from the military service. Truman fired MacArthur not just because he saw him as dead wrong about his prescription for American policy in Korea, Asia, and Europe more generally, but because he had defied and tried to usurp presidential authority in the making of foreign and military policies.[3]

As Truman later wrote in his *Memoirs,* "If there is one basic element in our Constitution, it is civilian control of the military. . . .

If I allowed him to defy the civil authorities in this manner, I myself would be violating my oath to uphold and defend the Constitution."[4] And as he later told Merle Miller in a more graphic description of his decision, "I didn't fire him because he was a dumb son of a bitch, although he was. . . . I fired him because he wouldn't respect the authority of the President." Truman also told Miller that he thought MacArthur at the age of seventy had lost his moorings or "wasn't right in the head." He had surrounded himself with "ass kissers . . . and there was never anybody around him to keep him in line."[5]

Although Truman understood that MacArthur's firing was going to raise a ruckus, he took comfort from the recollection that Abraham Lincoln had fired General George B. McClellan during the Civil War for failing to follow his orders and for issuing inappropriate political statements. "McClellan had political ambitions, which men in opposition to Lincoln sought to use," Truman observed, drawing a parallel to his Republican opposition, whom he saw as having fueled MacArthur's insubordination.

Truman justified his removal of MacArthur on three grounds: (a) the general had defied presidential directives to submit public statements for clearance before issuing them; (b) he had publicly disputed the president's foreign policy positions, undermining confidence in the president's authority with allies and adversaries; and (c) he had recklessly tried to turn the limited war in Korea into a full-scale conflict with the Chinese, risking a response from the Soviet Union that could have precipitated World War III.[6]

The public response to Truman's action was a combination of anger at the abrupt removal of a national hero from his military command, and less pronounced or subtle expressions of doubt about MacArthur's judgments and his fitness for political leadership or the presidency. Sixty-six percent of Americans disapproved of MacArthur's dismissal.[7]

"MacArthur's return was an amazing spectacle," Alonzo Hamby says. "Far from coming back in disgrace, the general arrived on American soil as a conquering hero." A crowd of perhaps 100,000 people greeted his arrival in Honolulu on April 16. The next day in San Francisco, 500,000 people lined the streets to catch a glimpse of the "conquering hero." Millions turned out to cheer as his motorcade proceeded through the financial district of New York on April

18. They showered him with 2,850 tons of ticker tape and confetti. "The parade," Hamby adds, "eclipsed the celebrations of Lindbergh's flight and Eisenhower's return from Europe."[8]

The Republicans invited MacArthur to address a joint session of Congress, which Truman and the Democratic majority felt they had no choice but to endorse. This gave MacArthur an opportunity to carry off one of the great acts of political theater in U.S. history. Squeezing every possible bit of advantage from the moment, MacArthur made his way down the aisle of the House chamber accompanied by senators and representatives eager to bask in his reflected glory. Standing at the rostrum in the well of the House, where presidents delivered their annual State of the Union speeches, MacArthur wrapped himself in the flag, denied any partisan intention, and proceeded to lambaste Truman's Korean and general foreign policies.

"I address you with neither rancor nor bitterness in the fading twilight of life," he declared, "with but one purpose in mind to serve my country." In his view, the administration's "appeasement" policy was a formula for national disaster. "Why, my soldiers asked of me, surrender military advantage to an enemy in the field." The implication was clear: Truman was leading the country toward defeat in Korea and around the world.

MacArthur ended with what the political scientist John Spanier said might be considered by some as "pure corn." "I am closing my 52 years of military service," MacArthur announced, and quoted from "the most popular barracks ballad" of his days at West Point: " 'Old soldiers never die; they just fade away.' And like the old soldier of that ballad, I now close my military career and just fade away — an old soldier who tried to do his duty as God gave him the light to see that duty. Good-by."

It was a memorable moment for members of Congress and millions of television viewers around the country. One congressman, carried away by his hero worship, declared: "We heard God speak here today, God in the flesh, the voice of God."[9]

One White House critic, who was offended by MacArthur's posturing and the overdrawn response to someone so transparently disrespectful of the president and the country's democratic traditions, joked that the general should have ridden to the Capitol on the back of an elephant, where he would have been greeted with the ceremonial burning of the Constitution, and the firing of a twenty-one-gun atom bomb salute. Truman privately called the speech "a hundred percent bullshit."

Yet for all the demonstrations of worshipful regard, the public mood was shifting. An increasing number of Americans were coming to view MacArthur as someone who was advocating unrealistic and dangerous policies that could lead the world into an apocalyptic conflict. When Gallup asked a cross section of Americans whether they thought MacArthur would make a good president, only 36 percent said yes, and 55 percent said no.

By July, as passions over MacArthur's dismissal cooled, 74 percent of Americans said they thought it was a "good idea" for the United Nations to agree to peace talks in Korea. The public reflected General Omar Bradley's view that the Korean conflict was "the wrong war, at the wrong place, at the wrong time, and with the wrong enemy."[10]

None of these doubts about MacArthur, however, benefited Truman. Predictably, Republican senators were scathing about the president's dismissal of someone they considered a legend. They called for the president's impeachment and denounced him as a stooge or possibly even a closet Communist. "This country today is in the hands of a secret inner coterie which is directed by agents of the Soviet Union," Senator William Jenner of Indiana implausibly declared. The *Chicago Tribune* urged the president's impeachment and conviction, saying that he "is unfit, morally and mentally for his high office."

While most Americans were not ready to endorse Jenner's wild accusation and see Truman as a traitor, they no longer had much confidence in the president. MacArthur's biographer William Manchester suggests that the public may have thought that Truman "had done the right thing, in this case avoiding the hazards of a general war, [but] in the wrong way." Instead of giving MacArthur the chance "to retire gracefully," he had fired him in a way that "seemed punitive, even indecent, and it violated all the traditions which the General cherished."[11] Republican congressmen inserted anti-Truman telegrams and letters from their constituents in the *Congressional Record:* the messages attacked the president as an "imbecile," "a pig," a "Judas," a "little ward politician," and a "red herring." Western Union wouldn't allow a woman to send a telegram to the White House calling the president "a moron."[12]

In May, six weeks after he had fired Mac-Arthur, Truman had only a 24 percent approval rating; a decisive 61 percent disapproved of his performance as president. Over the next three months, the ratings on his job performance remained stuck in the twenties.[13] But Truman was unfazed by this criticism. In his memoirs, he recalled that he expected the "wave of emotion" that MacArthur's return evoked in the country. He said, "It did not upset me." He refused to believe that the polls were the last word on his presidential performance. He wondered how Moses or Jesus Christ or Martin Luther would have behaved if they had taken polls in their respective times. "It isn't polls or public opinion alone of the moment that counts," he wrote a friend. "It is right and wrong, and leadership — men with fortitude, honesty and a belief in the right that make epochs in the history of the world." And as for the Republicans, who were demanding his impeachment, "They will find that they have a bear by the tail."[14]

The congressional hearings on Mac-Arthur's dismissal lasted forty-two days and compiled some 2.5 million words from thirteen witnesses, but Truman took considerable satisfaction from the fact that "nothing was turned up to give much encouragement to the domestic critics of the administration's policy." To the contrary, the hearings demonstrated the recklessness of MacArthur's advice in advocating an all-out war with China and possibly the Soviet Union as well.

During three days of testimony, McCullough points out, MacArthur sounded "self-absorbed and oddly disinterested in global issues. He would admit to no mistakes, no errors of judgment. . . . He belittled the danger of a larger conflict. But what if he happened to be wrong, he was asked. What if another world war resulted?" MacArthur said it would not be his fault. The burden of responsibility for global strategy rested with the Joint Chiefs. "To many," McCullough writes, "it seemed he had made the President's case."[15]

And if this weren't enough to convince observers of his irresponsibility in calling for an all-out attack on China, the subsequent testimony of Generals George Marshall and Omar Bradley and the other Joint Chiefs "refuted absolutely MacArthur's claim that they agreed with his strategy." Their appearance and statements before the committee "not only gave weight and validity to [the president's] decision, but discredited MacArthur in a way nothing else could have." Bradley later wrote that MacArthur's "legendary military pride had been hurt. The Red Chinese had made a fool of the infallible 'military genius.' " Carried away by personal animus toward the Communists, MacArthur wanted "an all-out war with Red China and possibly the Soviet Union, igniting World War III, and a nuclear holocaust."[16]

Nevertheless, MacArthur's lost standing did not raise Truman's, whose status was now irretrievably bound up with developments in Korea. He understood that as long as the war continued with increasing American casualties and no clear end in sight or belief that the sacrifices could be described as producing a victory, it would play havoc with his domestic approval.

In June, Truman had some hope that Moscow would be receptive to mediating an end to the conflict. After the Soviet ambassador to the UN announced his country's interest in arranging a cease-fire and China's official newspaper endorsed the proposal, the president declared his interest in discussions if they ended "aggression" and ensured South Korea's national security. In July, talks began at Kaesong, a city on the border between North and South

Korea. They collapsed in late August, but resumed again on October 25, in Panmunjom, another border city. A de facto ceasefire was reached by November 27, but talks now stalled over prisoner-of-war exchanges — whether there should be a one-for-one swap or, as the Chinese preferred, a repatriation of all captured forces, of which there were many more Chinese — 150,000 — than American or UN troops — about 16,000.

Truman's resistance to all-for-all was tied to a belief that many of the Chinese POWs left behind after a one-for-one exchange would not want to return to Communist China, and allowing these prisoners to choose would give the United States a propaganda victory at the end of the war, if not a battlefield one. It is not hard to imagine that he saw some gain for his political standing in such a victory. With more than a year to go in his term, a political resurgence could give him the wherewithal to make some substantive gains at home and abroad.

The year ended with the talks continuing but the outcome still uncertain even as casualties mounted. The war, which had settled into a series of ground battles between dug-in troops, reminded people of the awful, indecisive trench fighting of World War I. As a consequence, American frustration over the war mounted. In October, 56 percent of a survey agreed with one senator's description of the Korean conflict as "an utterly 'useless' war." By the middle of November, the skepticism about genuine Chinese interest in ending the war was reflected in the willingness of 41 percent of Americans to support the idea of using atom bombs, in one way or another, against "enemy targets in Korea."[17]

Truman himself had half a mind to make an end to the Korean fighting and the cold war with a decisive attack on the Communists. He confided to a diary a belief that the Communist governments were like the ruthless "head of a dope ring" toward whom the "proper approach now would be an ultimatum with a ten day expiration limit." Moscow should be told that "we intend to destroy every military base in Manchuria . . . and if there is any interference we shall eliminate any ports or cities necessary to accomplish our peaceful purposes. . . . We are tired of these phony calls for peace when there is no intention to make an honest approach to peace. . . . This means all out war." Truman then ticked off a list of cities in the Soviet Union and China that "will be eliminated. This is the final chance for the Soviet Government to decide whether it desires to survive or not."

Four months later, with the Korean War still unsettled, Truman wondered whether he should ask Moscow if it preferred to end the fighting or have "China and Siberia destroyed? You may have one or the other, whichever you want." This was a president venting his frustration over his powerlessness to end a limited war that was costing American blood and treasure and destroying his presidency. He had no intention of using the atomic bomb, but the fact that he could confide such thoughts, even to a private diary, is chilling.[18] As George Kennan would say later, no one — not even the most rational and humane of leaders — is to be trusted with these weapons of mass destruction. Kennan believed that civilization's preservation would ultimately depend on the abolition of such weapons by governments and nations everywhere.

As the war dragged on, Truman became more unpopular. In October, only 13 percent of Americans said they would like to see him elected in 1952. By year's end, Truman's approval rating had fallen to an all-time low of 23 percent.[19]

No political figure in the country did more

to sustain the negative views of the president and his administration than Senator Joseph McCarthy. He called Truman "a son of a bitch," said he should be impeached, and described him as drunk on "bourbon and Benedictine" when he decided to fire Mac-Arthur. At the same time, he lashed out at Dean Acheson, all but calling him a traitor: "You should not only resign from the State Department but you should remove yourself from the country and go to the nation for which you have been struggling and fighting so long."

In a June 1951 speech on the Senate floor, McCarthy savaged George Marshall, who had rejoined the administration in September 1950 as secretary of defense to help the president with the problems of the Korean War. McCarthy described Marshall as the principal culprit behind "a conspiracy so immense and an infamy so black as to dwarf any previous venture in the history of man." Senator William Jenner of Indiana attacked Marshall as "not only willing but eager to play the front man for traitors. The truth is this is no new role for him, for General George C. Marshall is a living lie."

These were astonishing accusations that in more rational times would have marked McCarthy and Jenner out as the crackpots they were, but these were not rational times. Many of their fellow senators were afraid of crossing McCarthy, having seen how the Wisconsin senator had destroyed Millard Tydings in the 1950 election.

For their part, neither Truman nor Marshall would answer McCarthy directly or, as Truman put it, "get down in the gutter with a gutter snipe." Marshall retired for the last time in September 1951, and the president would answer "no comment" when asked about McCarthy at press conferences.

It wasn't as if Truman was unmindful of the harm McCarthy was doing. One evening in 1951, he held a private meeting to ask some Democratic members of Congress and a handful of other men sympathetic to the president's dilemma what to do about McCarthy. When one senator suggested that they attack McCarthy through leaks to the press of ugly personal facts, Truman, slamming his hand on the table, rejected the proposal. "Nobody, not even the President of the United States, can approach too close to a skunk, in skunk territory, and expect to get anything out of it except a bad smell," Truman said. "If you think someone is telling a big lie about you," he added, "the only way to answer is with the whole truth."

Whether Truman could have done more

to rein in McCarthy is difficult to know. Senator Lyndon Johnson of Texas believed that Truman was wise to hold his fire and predicted that McCarthy would not be brought down until he overreached himself by attacking conservative institutions and individuals. This is what eventually happened in 1954, when McCarthy went after the army, and Johnson sprang to get him. During the army-McCarthy hearings, which Johnson arranged to have televised to show a mass audience how reckless and sinister McCarthy was, the Wisconsin senator destroyed himself with the sort of wild accusations that showed the public what a scoundrel and psychologically unbalanced man he truly was. In 1951, however, most Democrats, including Truman, did not think that the time was ripe for his downfall and that attacks by his known enemies, like the president, were more likely to reinforce the sympathies of his followers than diminish them.

This said, it is reasonable to argue that if Truman had publicly hit back against McCarthy and Jenner for what they said about Marshall, it might have undermined them more quickly. It remains difficult to grasp how any rational American could believe that George Marshall, who had been so much the architect of victory in World War II and so central a figure in the Truman administration's anti-Communist actions between 1945 and 1951, was anything but a loyal American. Truman did make broad public statements condemning irrational, distorted attacks, and without mentioning McCarthy or Jenner, comparing denunciations and slander to the sort of thing you see in Communist countries. But he wouldn't identify anyone directly as using these tactics. At a minimum, Truman might have encouraged respected leaders across the country to speak out in defense of Marshall in the hope of bringing a majority of Americans to censure McCarthy and Jenner for their irresponsible rhetoric.[20]

The successful negotiation and signing of a peace treaty with Japan in September 1951 was insufficient to combat the negative public feelings toward Truman and his administration over Korea and foreign affairs more generally. Where a large majority of Americans by 1951 had either friendly or neutral feelings toward the Japanese, an agreement that seemed to ensure that Japan would not be drawn into the Communist sphere and "gave the United States the right to maintain in Japan as much force as we wanted, anywhere we wanted, for as long as we wanted," in the words of John Foster Dulles, could not make up for public anger over the stalemate in Korea and the sense of vulnerability to Communist power around the globe.[21]

The fact that Truman had also been able to convince Dwight Eisenhower to take command of NATO forces in Europe in December 1950 should have given him some boost with the public. Not only was Eisenhower a more attractive national figure than MacArthur, but he also remained popular in Europe, which allowed him to build up NATO military strength to a point that he was confident of effectively countering a Soviet ground offensive by 1952. Despite these foreign affairs gains, the American public continued to see Truman as a poor leader who had jeopardized the country's safety. With the 1952 presidential election nearing, Americans were eager for a new president who seemed to know more about national security and how to defeat what most Americans saw as a worldwide Communist conspiracy.[22]

Truman's unpopularity also rested on the conviction that he was ineffective in domestic affairs. World Wars I and II had side-tracked progressivism and the New Deal, and now the Korean fighting stymied Truman's Fair Deal. Neither the public nor the Congress have ever found the wherewithal to focus on major reforms at home when the country seems to be battling for survival abroad.

By the summer of 1951, a substantial plurality of Americans — 45 percent — cited the economy, "the high cost of living," as their greatest concern. Truman did not help matters by pushing forward a program of economic controls comparable to what the government put in place during World War II. He called on Americans to sacrifice for the national well-being, declaring in June, "This is no time to yield to selfish interests who scorn equality of sacrifice."

But Truman's entreaties rang hollow. While shortages of consumer goods temporarily boosted inflation and accounted for the surge in concern about the economy, the situation in 1951 was nowhere near what it had been in 1943 or 1944, when economic controls were essential to manage a war economy. Truman's appeal for sacrifice and argument by invoking World War II was simply not convincing people and added to his diminished political influence.

A majority of Americans opposed increased economic restraints and higher taxes. They also thought that government expenditures were excessive and that Washington was spending itself into bankruptcy. These views were reflected in the passage of the Defense Production Act of 1951, which fell well short of Truman's requests for executive controls. He called the bill "the worst I ever had to sign," and predicted that it would produce severe inflation, which it never did. Similarly, he reluctantly signed the Revenue Act of 1951, which he believed fell well short of what the government needed to finance the war and the defense buildup he was pushing forward.[23]

Truman was also dogged by ongoing charges of corruption. An investigation led by Senator J. William Fulbright of Arkansas probed the Reconstruction Finance Corporation and influence peddling by White House aides. So did an exposé of corruption in the Internal Revenue Service by tax collectors tied to big-city Democratic machines, several of whom were convicted for taking bribes. These probes occurred against a backdrop of other investigations of organized crime and a scandal involving West Point cadets expelled for cheating on exams.

Although these investigations revealed more of "the appearance of wrongdoing" at the White House than any clear demonstrations of corruption, they nonetheless revived the earlier complaints about Truman as an architect of White House "cronyism" and as the former "senator from Pendergast." The allegations also gave the public reason to recall its earlier feelings that this was a man who had been unsuited for the presidency.[24]

9
LAST HURRAHS

In February 1951, Minnesota became the thirty-sixth state to ratify the Twenty-second Amendment to the Constitution, making it the law of the land that presidents could no longer be elected to more than two terms. Although many observers viewed this amendment as an act of revenge by the Republicans against Franklin Roosevelt, it muted the attack on Roosevelt's successor by excluding any sitting chief executive at the time of passage.

Consequently, Harry Truman could run for another term in 1952, and most Americans thought he would. Although 66 percent of Americans opposed giving him another term and trial heats pairing him against Eisenhower, Robert Taft, Earl Warren, and Harold Stassen showed him losing to all of them, 80 percent of a September 1951 survey and 58 percent of a January 1952 poll said he would be a candidate again.

Gallup never asked why people thought that someone so unpopular would decide to put himself before the voters in 1952.[1] But one can speculate that Truman's combativeness and determination to stand up to his opponents convinced people that he would not shy away from another contest with the Republicans for the White House.

In November 1951, however, a handful of administration insiders learned that the president had decided against running for another term. If a diary entry is to be trusted, Truman had made up his mind in April 1950. In a note to himself, he stated his intention not to seek his party's nomination in 1952. "In my opinion, eight years as President is enough and sometimes too much for any man to serve in that capacity," he wrote. "There is a lure to power. It can get into a man's blood just as gambling and lust for money have been known to do." He did not think a constitutional amendment was needed to convince him. "Custom based on the honor of the man in the office" should be sufficient to ensure against more than eight years as president.[2]

When he confided his decision to his staff in November of the following year, he asked them not to reveal it. He would make his intentions known in the spring of 1952.

Delaying an announcement meant he could keep people guessing and not become a lame duck until the closing months of his term.

Truman's resolve not to run again gave him a measure of freedom from pressure generated by the press and public opinion. However much he may have wished to boost his public approval ratings before he retired in January 1953, it was much less compelling than if he needed to ensure voter backing in another campaign.

His noncandidacy seems to have influenced his response to the corruption charges that dogged his administration throughout 1951 and 1952. The president was not indifferent to charges of wrongdoing against officeholders, as his removal of Democratic appointees serving as tax collectors around the country demonstrated. But he was slow to act against anyone he considered a friend who continued to enjoy his trust. He believed that some, if not much, of the agitation over questionable behavior was more the product of Republicans seeking political advantage in the next campaign than of actual misbehavior on the part of officials that he or Franklin Roosevelt had appointed. And even where there was some corner cutting by these Democrats, Truman believed it was no different from what Republicans had done with their patronage jobs.

The most notable case of the president's reluctance to fire a friend and supporter involved his attorney general, Howard J. McGrath. In 1949, after elevating Attorney General Tom Clark to the Supreme Court, an appointment he later described as his "biggest mistake" because he didn't like his decisions on the Court, Truman had appointed McGrath to succeed him. McGrath came with fine credentials — he had served as governor and senator from Rhode Island, solicitor general of the United States, and as the Democratic Party's national chairman, who had loyally backed the president in 1948. An added political consideration for Truman was that McGrath filled the president's need for a Catholic to serve in the cabinet or some other high administration post.

McGrath's reputation as a heavy drinker and a lazy man who left the responsibilities of his various offices to subordinates did not deter Truman from making him attorney general, a high-visibility position in which someone with McGrath's limitations could embarrass the president. Truman's affinity for handing out jobs to political and personal associates with questionable credentials was a problem that dogged him throughout his tenure.

By late 1951 Truman had begun to have regrets about the McGrath appointment. A private unsigned memo to the president described the Justice Department, "once far and away the best legal institution in the United States," as "now verging on the third rate." The department was "a headless juggernaut." McGrath's inattentiveness to department business conducted by deputies, who were largely unqualified political appointees, had reduced the Justice Department's effectiveness and embarrassed the White House.

In December, Truman had decided to cross party lines and replace McGrath with Wayne Morse, a Republican senator from Oregon, a man known for his integrity and independence, but Morse turned him down. Truman then considered appointing Justin V. Miller, a prominent attorney with impeccable credentials. But apparently, pressure from J. Edgar Hoover over negative comments Miller had made publicly about the FBI decided Truman against nominating him; he had enough trouble with conservatives over Korea and accusations of coddling Communists without turning Hoover against him. At the same time, McGrath was refusing to resign, and he was supported by leading Catholics and by Rhode Island senator Theodore Green, a Democratic Party mainstay. With few other options, Truman invited McGrath to take responsibility for cleaning up his department by replacing political operatives under suspicion of corruption with qualified attorneys.

McGrath responded by asking Newbold Morris, a New York Republican reformer, to take charge of an independent investigation. Morris agreed and at once asserted his independence by insisting that all officeholders making more than ten thousand dollars a year complete a questionnaire revealing their assets and outside income. This demand angered McGrath, who convinced Truman that it would be an unwarranted invasion of privacy. But then McGrath took a step too far by deciding to fire Morris without White House approval. When this news was announced, Truman felt compelled to demand McGrath's resignation. Truman then appointed James McGranery, a well-respected federal judge, as attorney general, but he could not get the nomination through the Senate for more than two months. During that time, the

Justice Department's internal housecleaning largely ground to a halt.

The public airing of Truman's problems with McGrath and the charges of uninvestigated incompetence and possible corruption in the Justice Department strengthened feelings in the country that the president and his party had been in power too long and that it was time for a change in Washington. Truman hoped that by the time November rolled around his new attorney general might have restored public faith in the Justice Department and muted the corruption issue in the campaign.[3]

Another round of labor troubles, however, canceled out whatever surge in approval Truman hoped might develop. The president's largest concern at the start of 1952 was the threat of a steelworkers' strike that would shut down the most important American defense industries. In March, when the government's Wage Stabilization Board recommended a hefty 26-cent-an-hour wage increase for workers, the steel producers demanded a $12-a-ton increase to offset the higher costs. Truman encouraged the steel companies to settle for $4.50, pointing out that they were enjoying great profits from Korean War production and that any greater increase in steel prices would play havoc with administration efforts to hold down inflation.

Big steel rejected Truman's advice, and the unions set a strike deadline for April 9. The president could invoke the Taft-Hartley law to compel an eighty-day cooling-off period, but Truman saw this as confirming the validity of the antilabor measure that had passed Congress over his veto. He had no desire to give Taft a boost toward a presidential nomination in 1952, nor did he wish to antagonize labor, which he saw as vital to Democratic chances of holding on to the White House and control of Congress. Moreover, he had little sympathy for the steel producers, who he believed were being greedy and unpatriotic in their refusal to settle the dispute.

With a strike now all too certain, he saw no better alternative than to order a government seizure of the steel companies under his inherent powers as commander in chief in wartime. He accepted Secretary of Defense Robert Lovett's assessment that "any stoppage of steel production, for even a short time, would increase the risk we had taken in the 'stretch-out' of the armament program." In Korea, Lovett also told him, "we are holding the line with ammunition and not with the lives of our troops. Any curtailment of steel production . . . would endanger the lives of our men."

Truman understood that seizing the steel mills would provoke a constitutional controversy over presidential power. But he rationalized his decision by recalling that Abraham Lincoln, Woodrow Wilson, and Franklin Delano Roosevelt had all used their inherent powers to ensure the national security. Moreover, he had a 1949 memo from then attorney general and now associate justice Tom Clark confirming the president's power to take such action. More important, Chief Justice Fred Vinson, who was a close friend and fellow poker player, had privately endorsed the president's right to seize the steel companies and encouraged him to believe that a majority of the Supreme Court would support that opinion.

It is also reasonable to believe that Truman's decision to seize the companies partly rested on a personal desire to combat a sense of powerlessness that had settled over him in the spring of 1952. His aides saw him as demoralized and exhausted. He was so pale, strained, and tired that they feared he was on the verge of a collapse. His low approval ratings, his inability to bring the Korean War to an end, and the persistence of corruption allegations within his administration led him to feel that he was no longer an effective chief executive. For Truman, seizing the steel companies was not only a way to serve the national interest but also a decisive action that reaffirmed his relevance as president.

It proved to be one of the greatest blunders of his presidency. Truman was vilified in the media and in the Congress as a Hitler, a Mussolini, a president who had abused his constitutional powers and should be impeached for trying to set up a dictatorship.

The steel companies at once sued the government for violating their property rights. In response, Judge David Pine of the U.S. district court issued a stay that declared the president's action "illegal and without the authority of law." And to Truman's great dismay, on June 2 the Supreme Court endorsed Pine's ruling by a 6–3 vote. All nine justices were Roosevelt and Truman appointees and it mystified Truman that so liberal a court would overturn his executive order. The majority opinion declared that the commander in chief could not seize private property to prevent a strike impeding production. "This is a job for the Nation's lawmakers, not for its military authorities," the majority opinion declared.

William O. Douglas, explaining why the liberal justices had issued their ruling, said, "Tomorrow another President might use the same power to prevent a wage increase, to curb trade unionists, to regiment labor as oppressively as industry thinks it has been regimented by this seizure."

The Court's decision produced a labor walkout that lasted fifty-three days and resulted in a twenty-one-million-ton reduction in steel output and $400 million in lost wages. Although Lovett would complain that "no enemy nation could have so crippled our production as has this work stoppage," the strike did not actually have any significant impact on the Korean fighting.

Nor did it significantly undermine the national economy. The settlement in July, which gave labor a wage increase of 21 cents an hour and steel producers an additional $5.20 a ton, was much like what could have been agreed to in March. Instead, the country suffered through a bitter labor-management dispute, which took an additional toll on the president's standing. Only a third of the public agreed with his seizure of the steel mills, and Truman went into a blue funk over the Court's decision that further diminished his energy to deal with the problems troubling the last months of his presidency.[4]

Although Truman would put a positive face on his Korean War policies during 1952, his frustration over the stalemate deepened. The sticking point in negotiations with the Communists remained the exchange of POWs. Recalling the forced repatriation of Soviet prisoners from Germany after World War II that provoked some suicides and "slave labor" for most of those who were compelled to return, Truman was determined to avoid that sort of unprincipled settlement. "We will not buy an armistice by turning over human beings for slaughter or slavery," he said in a speech at West Point in May 1952. It would be like "trafficking in human slavery."

Of the approximately 116,000 Communist POWs, only 83,000 were willing to return to China and North Korea. Truman declared "voluntary repatriation" a nonnegotiable principle that would have to be part of any armistice agreement. The Communists were as unyielding: any settlement would have to include an all-for-all provision on POWs. Although they asserted that the U.S. estimate of 116,000 POWs was a deliberate undercount, which allowed the Americans to brainwash some of their troops into staying behind, they would settle for the 116,000 count as an unacknowledged concession that could help end the fighting.

For Truman, giving in on "voluntary repatriation" or accepting a one-for-one formula would have meant a victory for the Communists, and he was determined to have something more than the restoration of South Korea's autonomy at the end of the fighting. He wished to tie the loss of so many thousands of American lives to some larger gain in the worldwide conflict with the Communists. He believed that the refusal of some thirty-five thousand Communist troops to return to China and North Korea could give him and the United States "a 'psychological' Cold War victory at home and abroad."

In June, Truman agreed to a bombing campaign against the Communists that he hoped would force them into an armistice. In the closing days of the month, U.S. bombers struck hydroelectric plants along the Yalu River that deprived North Korea and Manchuria of electric power. Two weeks later, air attacks on Pyongyang inflicted heavy damage on the North Korean capital. When these actions produced no movement in the negotiations, Truman approved air attacks on military installations in northeast Korea near the Chinese and Soviet borders.

In September, the White House coupled the bombings with an increase in the number of POWs it offered to return from 70,000 to 83,000, which was the number it had identified as preferring repatriation. The Chinese insisted on 100,000 to 110,000, including all their POWs. They were willing to leave only North Korean prisoners behind. By the end of September, it was clear that neither side would meet the other's demands, and in October the armistice talks had reached a seemingly unbridgeable impasse. In December, a United Nations proposal for an exchange of prisoners that placed POWs resisting repatriation in its care won American support but was rejected by the Communists.[5]

In the closing months of his administration, Truman's greatest hope for the vindication of his presidency was a Democratic victory in the 1952 presidential and congressional elections. In the spring, he believed that the isolationist senator Robert Taft of Ohio would be the Republican nominee, and for patriotic and personal reasons he was more than eager to see Taft defeated. He urged his friend Chief Justice Fred Vinson to run, and when Vinson refused, he put out feelers to General Eisenhower.

Eisenhower had no interest in becoming a Democratic candidate. Nor did he have much regard for Truman, whose commitments to the New Deal and the Fair Deal were at odds with his more restricted view of federal activism. In December 1951, the president wrote to the general, saying that he was eager to return to Missouri, but wished to "keep the isolationists out of the White House," meaning Taft. "I wish you would let me know what you intend to do. It will be between us and no one else."

Eisenhower replied on January 1 that he also wanted to retire from public life but acknowledged that this could be preempted by "a conviction of duty." He said he had no intention of seeking a nomination and declared, "The possibility that I will ever be drawn into political activity is so remote as to be negligible." Only "extraordinary circumstances" could change his mind. Yet on January 6, the Massachusetts Republican senator Henry Cabot Lodge announced in Washington that he was heading an Eisenhower-for-president committee, which was launching the general's campaign by running him in the New Hampshire primary.

The following day, Eisenhower publicly restated the reluctance he had expressed to Truman about seeking the presidency, but he left no doubt that he did not object to Lodge's efforts. Truman was angry that Eisenhower refused to take up his suggestion of a Democratic Party draft but was receptive to a Republican one. At a news conference, when pressed for a comment on the general's implicit willingness to run for the Republican nomination, Truman snidely replied: "I don't want to stand in his way at all, because I think very highly of him, and if he wants to get out and have all the mud and rotten eggs and rotten tomatoes thrown at him, that is his business." Privately, Truman told some of his aides, "I'm sorry to see these fellows get Ike into this business. They're showing him gates of gold and silver which will turn out copper and tin."

If Eisenhower had chosen to run as a Democrat, Truman would have been more than happy to make the same promises of "gold and silver" and to expose him to all the rotten stuff opponents had tossed at him and would, Truman believed, throw at any candidate.

With Vinson refusing to seek the nomination and with Eisenhower and Taft the leading Republican candidates, Truman tried to convince Governor Adlai Stevenson of Illinois to run, in large part because he was unhappy with the possibility that Senator Estes Kefauver of Tennessee might win the nomination. Truman had a visceral dislike of Kefauver, whose investigations of organized crime and government corruption, including corruption in the Truman administration, had projected him into the national spotlight. Truman preferred Averell Harriman, whose extensive background in diplomacy and identification with both Roosevelt and Truman made him a potentially strong candidate. But Harriman had never run for an elected office, and it seemed a stretch to make his first contest a bid for the presidency.

By contrast, Stevenson had won a landslide vote four years earlier in Illinois, a large midwestern swing state. Truman also liked what Stevenson had been saying publicly about government policies and was confident he had the right political feel to be an effective candidate and a successful president. In a January 1952 meeting at the White House, he apparently told Stevenson, "If a knucklehead like me can be President and not do too badly, think what a really educated smart guy like you [a Princeton graduate] could do in the job."

Stevenson appreciated Truman's confidence in him but refused his offer of support. Stevenson was not sure that 1952 was a good time to run as a Democrat. He believed that it was likely to be a Republican year after five Democratic terms and that, even if he chose to run, it would be a poor idea to be Truman's handpicked successor. He considered Truman currently more of a liability than a help to any Democrat.

Truman gave some consideration to endorsing a "draft Truman" campaign, and a New Hampshire man entered the president's name in the state's primary. When the president declared himself a noncandidate and the publisher of the state's leading newspaper, the *Manchester Union Leader,* chided him for not running, Truman left his name on the ballot. Although he didn't think that state primaries counted for much alongside of the influence exerted by state party bosses at nominating conventions, his defeat in New Hampshire on March 11 by Kefauver was a sobering reminder of his diminished electoral appeal. On March 29, eighteen days after his drubbing in New Hampshire, Truman definitively announced that he wouldn't run again.

He put renewed pressure on Stevenson to

become a candidate, but the governor said he wanted to run for reelection in Illinois and wouldn't commit himself to a presidential campaign. At the beginning of July, the Republicans nominated Eisenhower on the first ballot, making Truman all the more determined to find a strong Democratic nominee. He was convinced that Eisenhower was too inexperienced to be an effective political leader and that the Taft Republicans would wield the real power in an Eisenhower administration and return the country to isolationism.

As the Democratic convention scheduled for Chicago in late July neared, the only Democrat Truman saw to support was his vice president, Alben Barkley. He was eager to run, but at seventy-four he would be the oldest man ever elected president and labor leaders shot down his candidacy as a bad idea.

As the convention began, Stevenson coyly asked Truman whether he would object if he allowed himself to become a candidate. Truman was delighted with Stevenson's decision and asked Harriman, who had become a contender and enjoyed support from more than a hundred delegates, to withdraw in favor of Stevenson. When Harriman agreed and Truman lobbied other

251

Democratic leaders to line up behind Stevenson, the governor, having given a stirring welcoming speech to the convention, overcame a Kefauver first-ballot lead to win nomination on the third roll call. As a gesture to southern delegates, who were largely alienated from Truman's White House, Stevenson selected Senator John Sparkman of Alabama as his running mate.

Stevenson launched his campaign at once by overtly taking his distance from Truman. He declared himself indebted to no one for his nomination; replaced Truman's Democratic National Committee chairman with his own man; appointed a campaign manager who had no ties to the White House; set up his campaign headquarters in Springfield, Illinois, rather than in Washington; told an Oregon newspaper that he hoped to "clean up the mess in Washington"; and did not object to Sparkman's published comment that Truman had mishandled the steel strike.

Truman dashed off a letter to Stevenson that he never sent, but which gave expression to his anger at being shoved aside by the man he had helped and believed he could make president. "It seems to me that the Presidential Nominee and his running-mate are trying to beat the Democratic

President instead of the Republicans," he wrote. ". . . There is no mess in Washington. . . . When you say that you are indebted to no one for your nomination, that makes nice reading in the sabotage press, but gets you no votes because it isn't true. . . . I'm telling you to take your crackpots, your high socialites with their noses in the air, run your campaign and win if you can. Cowfever [Kefauver] could not have treated me any more shabbily than have you." When asked at an August 21 press conference how he felt about the Stevenson-Sparkman campaign, he sat on his anger but his "no comment" spoke volumes.

Truman refused to accept that, whatever history's judgment on his presidency, current opinion about his performance was largely negative. He prided himself on being a much shrewder politician than Stevenson, and while this may have been generally true, in 1952 Stevenson read the public's mood more clearly than the president. Except for die-hard Democrats devoted to New Deal–Fair Deal programs and retaining affection for the two presidents identified with them, a majority of voters were eager for a change, especially in the Korean War, which Americans decisively wanted to end.

The campaign became one of the nastiest

in the country's history. Deprived of the presidency since 1932 and seeing the country as ready for a political shift, a unified Republican Party, led by Eisenhower and his running mate, Richard Nixon, enthusiastically vilified the Democrats. Calling 1952 a "Time for Change," the Republicans hammered on Truman's alleged record of failures: described in shorthand as K1C2 — Korea, communism, and corruption.

Eisenhower took a relatively high road in attacking the culture of "crooks and cronies," who had given us "the mess in Washington." He promised to replace the Fair Deal with an "Honest Deal." But understanding that the Democrats were vulnerable to harsher attacks, he gave second place on the ticket to Nixon, whose reputation for smear tactics and anticommunism made him an ideal running mate in 1952.

Nixon was the perfect hatchet man, describing Truman and Acheson as "traitors to the high principles in which many of the nation's Democrats believe." Stevenson, Nixon said, held "a Ph.D. from Dean Acheson's Cowardly College of Communist Containment." It was time for "rollback and liberation" rather than Truman's failed fight against Communist domination of Eastern

Europe and China that marred his foreign policy.

Eisenhower joined the attack with complaints about twenty years of Communist appeasement by fellow travelers in Washington. In Wisconsin, with Joe McCarthy on the platform, Eisenhower endorsed his anti-Communist crusade, if not his methods, and deleted from his speech several complimentary references to George Marshall. On October 24, Eisenhower sealed his almost certain victory by promising to end the Korean conflict — "the burial ground for twenty thousand American dead" — by going to Korea.

Whatever his anger at Stevenson, Truman shelved it to engage in another whistle-stop campaign in which he struck back at Eisenhower and the Republicans. He was justifiably enraged by the exaggerated accusations about his administration's weak response to Communist aggression and the vague promises about "honorably" ending the Korean War by going to Korea. He was especially offended by Eisenhower's deletion of positive comments about Marshall — the man "responsible for his whole career" — calling it "shameful" and wondering how anyone could "stoop so low." He excoriated Eisenhower's rejection of a foreign policy he had helped construct and doubted that he could possibly be an effective president. He over-reached, however, when he attacked Eisenhower for turning a blind eye to the "sinister forces . . . Anti-Semitism, Anti-Catholicism and anti-foreignism" that "have hidden themselves within the Republican Party for years." In striking out at Eisenhower and Nixon, Truman was hoping not only to secure a Stevenson victory but also to serve his own historical reputation.

Eisenhower was so incensed at Truman's remarks about his accommodation to "sinister forces" that he said, "I'll never ride down Pennsylvania Avenue with him! I'll meet him at the Capitol steps. Just how low can you get?"

This time there were no surprises or upsets. The country resoundingly declared, "I like Ike." Eisenhower decisively beat Stevenson by 6.6 million out of 61 million popular votes. The margin in the Electoral College favored Eisenhower by fivefold — 442 to 89. He won thirty-nine of the forty-eight states, including Stevenson's Illinois and Truman's Missouri. Both houses of Congress also went to the Republicans, though by narrow margins.[6]

It was a shattering end to the Truman presidency. But, as with so many other times in his life, Truman would respond sensibly to the defeat. Mindful of the country's traditions and of the need to show the world the virtues of America's democratic system, he did all he could to make the transition to Eisenhower and the opposition party as uneventful as possible. He did not wish to see a repetition of the strained transition from Herbert Hoover to Franklin Roosevelt in 1933. But Truman's differences with Eisenhower eclipsed his good intentions. The president-elect was correct but unfriendly in the one meeting he had with Truman on November 18. (Truman described Eisenhower as "frozen grimness throughout.") Truman reciprocated the coolness by publicly describing Eisenhower's trip to Korea in December as "a piece of demagoguery." Their brief time together riding to Eisenhower's inauguration demonstrated how much they disliked each other: Eisenhower refused to make the customary visit to the Oval Office to pay his respects to the outgoing president, and Truman pointedly told Eisenhower that he was not at his inaugural in 1949 because he wasn't invited.[7]

Truman's last weeks in office were devoted to public and private reminiscing about his accomplishments as president. In a farewell address on January 15, he reviewed his administration's gains and predicted the eventual collapse of the Soviet Union. He asserted that his containment policy would win the cold war. "Nobody can say for sure when that is going to be, or exactly how it will come about. . . . Whether the Communist rulers shift their policies of their own free will — or whether the change comes about in some other way — I have no doubt in the world that a change will occur," he said. His prediction was impressively prescient.[8]

As his term came to an end, Truman took comfort in public demonstrations of affection for him. At Union Station, where he, Bess, and Margaret boarded a train on January 20, 1953, to take them home to Independence, thousands of people saw them off. Even larger crowds greeted their return home. The public regard, Truman confided to a diary, "was the pay-off for thirty years of hell and hard work."[9]

EPILOGUE

Sixty-eight years old and in good health when he left the White House in January 1953, Harry Truman lived for almost twenty more years. And although in time he would recede from the minds of most Americans, he never entirely fell from view. He was too strong a personality and too devoted to the national interest to remove himself totally from public deliberations.[1]

In the first years after leaving office, he remained an outspoken partisan. He disliked Dwight Eisenhower and his conservative economic policies and took every opportunity to denounce them as throwbacks to the bad old pre–New Deal days. He saw Eisenhower as the captive of big business interests more intent on serving themselves than the national well-being. His tensions with the Eisenhower administration were so intense that he refused to attend a White House dinner in 1959 honoring Winston

Churchill, for whom he continued to have the highest regard.

Truman's antagonism to Eisenhower and the Republicans moved him to actively oppose them in the 1956 election. Believing that Adlai Stevenson would be no more successful than he had been in 1952, Truman publicly supported New York governor Averell Harriman for the Democratic presidential nomination. But when Stevenson became the party's nominee and made Estes Kefauver his running mate, Truman muted his differences with both men by endorsing the ticket and campaigning for them in the fall.

Eisenhower's reelection by a wide margin frustrated Truman, but he took pleasure in continuing Democratic Party control of the House and the Senate. When a recession and traditional midterm losses for the party controlling the White House made 1958 look like a good year for the Democrats, Truman threw himself into the political struggle for congressional dominance. Refusing to accept that at seventy-four he might not be able to stand the rigors of another campaign, he spoke in twenty states for the party's candidates. Democratic victories expanded the party's margin in the Senate to a lopsided sixty-four to thirty-four and increased the advantage in the House to nearly two to one. The gains hugely pleased him.

The 1960 election impressed Truman as a great opportunity for the Democrats to regain the presidency. Eisenhower's second term had been a period of setbacks in the cold war: the Soviets' success in launching *Sputnik,* the first satellite to orbit the earth, in October 1957, gave Moscow an apparent advantage in intercontinental ballistic missiles; and a U.S. spy plane, the U-2, was shot down over the Soviet Union in May 1960, which scuttled a summit meeting between Eisenhower and Nikita Khrushchev. Moreover, continuing domestic difficulties with the economy made the Republicans vulnerable to defeat.

Truman worried, however, that the candidacy of Senator John F. Kennedy of Massachusetts would jeopardize the Democrats' chances. He believed that Kennedy at forty-three was too young and inexperienced and that his Catholic identity would lead to his likely defeat in November, resulting in Vice President Richard Nixon's election as president. Because he despised Nixon as an unprincipled opportunist who had questioned his patriotism, Truman felt compelled to oppose Kennedy openly. He also feared the influence of Kennedy's father, Joseph Kennedy, whose affinity for isolationist foreign policies, antagonism to Franklin Roosevelt, and support of Joseph McCarthy made Truman eager to keep him as far from the White House as possible. "It's not the Pope I'm afraid of," Truman said. "It's the pop."[2]

In May, after Kennedy had won a crucial primary in West Virginia that made him the front-runner for the Democratic nomination, Truman endorsed Stuart Symington, the senior senator from Missouri, and hoped that he or Senate Majority Leader Lyndon Johnson of Texas would become the party's nominee. In July, on the eve of the convention, with Kennedy the predicted winner, Truman held a press conference to complain that the convention was "rigged" in Kennedy's favor and urged Kennedy to stand aside until he was experienced enough to deal with the crucial foreign policy challenges certain to face the next president. Truman also announced that he would not attend the convention in Los Angeles as a protest against the machinations that seemed to have settled the outcome before the delegates met.

Although Truman's public opposition offended Kennedy and his supporters, it was ineffective. To win Truman's support and unite the Democratic Party, Kennedy followed his nomination by placing a placating phone call to the former president. Flattered by the attention and as eager as ever to beat Nixon, Truman readily agreed to help in the campaign. Kennedy then cemented Truman's backing with a visit to Independence for a face-to-face meeting. Truman followed through on promises to speak for Kennedy by traveling to nine states, where he gave thirteen speeches and put in long days that would have exhausted someone much younger than seventy-six years old.

After his election, Kennedy won Truman's enthusiastic approval by making public demonstrations of personal regard for the party's senior statesman. An invitation to meet with Kennedy in the Oval Office the day after his inauguration and a formal dinner in November 1961 to honor Truman, who had never been invited to the White House during Eisenhower's eight years, relieved some of Truman's doubts about the young man's suitability for the presidency. Kennedy's support of domestic initiatives that echoed Truman's earlier proposals for national health insurance, federal aid to education, and civil rights endeared him as well. More important, Kennedy's success in resolving the Cuban Missile Crisis in 1962 persuaded Truman that Kennedy was entirely worthy of the office.

Nineteen sixty was Truman's last major participation in a political campaign. He had involved himself against the advice of his wife and daughter. Bess had urged him to leave current political battles to younger men. When Margaret had told him that he was just like his two-year-old grandson, Truman said: "He runs all the time, never walks, and talks all the time and never says anything."[3]

Kennedy's election persuaded Truman to move to the political sidelines. This did not preclude ceremonial occasions such as attending Kennedy's funeral in 1963. Nor one in 1965, when Lyndon Johnson came to Independence to sign a Medicare bill, which was seen as a significant advance toward Truman's unfulfilled proposal for national health insurance. Nor did it preclude an address to the Senate on his eightieth birthday when Democrats and Republicans alike paid Truman tributes that brought tears to his eyes.

While he curbed his public partisanship, he was not ready to hold his tongue in private. In 1961, he began a series of conversations with the journalist Merle Miller that they agreed would not be published as a book until after the president had died. Truman was scathing about his enemies and endearingly candid. Some of what he said was simply not true: Miller, quoting Mark Twain, said, "He told the truth, mainly. There were things which he stretched, but mainly he told the truth." Truman had no qualms about embellishing some of his recollections. He quoted an old-time Missouri politician: "Goddamn an eyewitness, he always spoils a good story."[4] Hamby described Miller's Truman as "a crusty old man who said what he thought and exemplified the best in traditional American values."[5]

When Truman left the White House, however much he welcomed the release from the daily grind of being president, he had worried that the retreat into private life might leave him frustrated and unhappy. But he quickly learned that a former president can find satisfying work without the constant pressure of the office.

There was the pleasure of being back in Independence among family and old friends. There was also the constant demand for appearances that he selectively chose to fill or reject, as he liked. Offers of business ventures, which he resisted as an improper use of his celebrity, were a constant temptation for someone who had no government pension, for his service either in the Senate or as president, and only modest savings. But the sale of the family farm, a book contract for his memoirs that paid him $600,000 over five years, and a presidential pension approved by Congress in 1958 gave him a substantial measure of financial security.

Between 1953 and 1956, the production of his memoirs principally occupied Truman's time, though it was not very satisfying. Understanding that he needed a lot of help to reconstruct his prepresidential and presidential years, he relied on several ghostwriters and researchers. In addition, eager to offer an idealized picture of himself and his eight years in the White House, the memoirs became more a kind of state paper than the reflections of a life-and-blood character whose real persona was far more interesting than the one portrayed in the books. Because the manuscript ran to 500,000 words, Doubleday decided to publish the book in two volumes, the first in 1955 and the second the following year. Although reviewers would complain about the antiseptic, self-serving, and sometimes inaccurate substance of the memoirs, they also complimented Truman on doing what most presidents had shunned — providing a detailed recounting of their presidential years.

Truman took far more pleasure in creating a presidential library and museum in Independence. Following the Franklin Roosevelt model in Hyde Park, New York, Truman oversaw the building of a modest but dignified structure to house his personal and presidential papers and recount his White House history in museum exhibits. The private fund-raising to construct the facility and the transfer of papers and artifacts, which began in 1950, took seven years. The library and museum opened in July 1957 with Eleanor Roosevelt, former president Herbert Hoover (who was building his own library in Iowa), Dean Acheson, and other dignitaries present. Like the Roosevelt Library, the Truman facility was put under the control of the National Archives, though Truman continued to have a final say on the timing and content of record openings.

The chief justice of the United States, Earl Warren, addressed the approximately five thousand people who attended the opening-day ceremony and celebrated the occasion as a landmark moment in the preservation of the records of a major presidential administration. Initially, however, Truman, who occupied an office in the library and kept close track of developing research projects relying on the library's collections, held back the release of the most revealing documents relating to both his prepresidential and presidential careers. It would take some thirty years after the library was opened and several years after Truman had passed away before the richest material became available. To his credit, however, Truman's regard for history eventually gave scholars the opportunity to study his administration in depth. Moreover, he successfully lobbied Congress to appropriate funds to put all presidential papers, which were scattered in different locations around the country, on microfilm.

Truman's decision to return to Independence, where he lived modestly in the family's unpretentious house and walked the mile to his library most mornings, gave him a renewed appeal to a majority of Americans. His refusal to exploit his standing as a former president by identifying himself with commercial enterprises also encouraged views of him as someone more intent on preserving the dignity of his office than on making a lot of money. His outspokenness, punctuated by down-home phrases, reminded folks of why they had rallied to him in 1948.

National and international developments also made him seem sensible and attractive. Lyndon Johnson's Great Society gave life to a number of reforms Truman had tried to enact as part of his Fair Deal, vindicating Truman's judgment on what the country needed to improve the lives of most Americans. At the same time, Johnson's failed war in Vietnam reminded people of the frustrations Truman had experienced over Korea. But, more important, Johnson's evasive actions in escalating the war undermined public trust, opening up what was described as a credibility gap. Truman's "plain speaking," as Miller titled his book, added to a renewed regard for Truman as a president who squared with the people and took direct responsibility for his actions. This side of Truman's character became even more appealing during Nixon's Watergate scandal. A presidential cover-up of wrongdoing that became apparent with the release of White House tapes and forced Nixon's resignation spurred a longing for a president like Truman whose integrity stood in marked contrast to Nixon's dishonesty.

By 1991, the collapse of the Soviet Union had vindicated Truman's judgment on the wisdom of containing rather than fighting an all-out war with the Communists, as MacArthur had urged. His contribution to victory in the cold war without a devastating nuclear conflict elevated him to the stature of a great or near-great president.

The publication in 1992 of David McCullough's highly flattering thousand-page biography of Truman deepened the conviction among millions of Americans that Harry Truman was a special president who deserved to be remembered in a league with Theodore Roosevelt, Woodrow Wilson, and Franklin Roosevelt as the best modern occupants of the White House.

The ancient Greeks believed that fate is character. Truman's current standing as an up-by-the-bootstraps American whose fortuitous elevation to the presidency and ultimate good sense and honesty in leading the nation through perilous times are a demonstration of how circumstances and human decency can ultimately produce a successful life — and a presidency that resonates as a model of how someone can acquit himself in the highest office. Truman's life and public record give continuing hope that Lincoln's view of America as the last best hope of earth may remain a viable standard by which the country can still aim to live.

NOTES

1: Preludes

1. Margaret Truman, ed., *Where the Buck Stops: The Personal and Private Writings of Harry S. Truman* (New York: Warner Books, 1989), 1.
2. Alonzo L. Hamby, *Man of the People: A Life of Harry S. Truman* (New York: Oxford University Press, 1995), 3.
3. Thomas Wolfe, *You Can't Go Home Again* (New York: Harper and Brothers, 1940), 508.
4. Hamby, *Man of the People,* 8–9.
5. Harry S. Truman, *Memoirs of Harry S. Truman,* vol. 1, *Year of Decisions* (New York: Doubleday, 1955), 119–20.
6. Harry S. Truman, *The Autobiography of Harry S. Truman* (Columbia: University of Missouri Press, 2002), 41.
7. David McCullough, *Truman* (New York: Simon & Schuster, 1992), 89–90.

8. Ibid., 63.
9. Hamby, *Man of the People,* 15, 58.
10. McCullough, *Truman,* 113–35; Hamby, *Man of the People,* 66–82.
11. Hamby, *Man of the People,* 94–100.
12. McCullough, *Truman,* 158–66.
13. Hamby, *Man of the People,* 86.
14. Ibid., 101–14.
15. McCullough, *Truman,* 166–71; Hamby, *Man of the People,* 115–31.
16. McCullough, *Truman,* 171–73; Hamby, *Man of the People,* 145–47.
17. McCullough, *Truman,* 173–92.
18. Ibid.
19. Ibid., 193–95, 201–4. Also see, H. Truman, *Autobiography of Harry S. Truman,* 67.
20. H. Truman, *Autobiography of Harry S. Truman,* 67–68; McCullough, *Truman,* 204–12; Hamby, *Man of the People,* 188–99.
21. Hamby, *Man of the People,* 198.
22. H. Truman, *Memoirs,* vol. 1, 142.
23. Hamby, *Man of the People,* 199.
24. McCullough, *Truman,* 214.
25. Ibid., 213–34.
26. Ibid., 217.
27. Hamby, *Man of the People,* 200–27.
28. McCullough, *Truman,* 239.
29. Hamby, *Man of the People,* 235.

30. McCullough, *Truman,* 241–52; Hamby, *Man of the People,* 228–47.

31. McCullough, *Truman,* 253–91; Hamby, *Man of the People,* 248–60.

32. James MacGregor Burns, *Roosevelt: The Soldier of Freedom* (New York: Harcourt Brace Jovanovich, 1970), 503–6.

33. Hamby, *Man of the People,* 278.

34. McCullough, *Truman,* 294.

35. Ibid., 320.

36. Arthur M. Schlesinger Jr., *The Cycles of American History* (Boston: Houghton Mifflin, 1989), 337–42.

37. McCullough, *Truman,* 333–42.

38. Ibid., 339.

39. Robert Dallek, *Franklin D. Roosevelt and American Foreign Policy, 1932–1945* (New York: Oxford University Press, 1995), 519.

40. McCullough, *Truman,* 342; Hamby, *Man of the People,* 286–90.

41. Hamby, *Man of the People,* 293.

2: ENDING THE WAR AND PLANNING THE PEACE

1. Alben Barkley, *That Reminds Me — The Autobiography of the Veep* (Garden City, N.Y.: Doubleday, 1954), 197.

2. George H. Gallup, *The Gallup Poll, 1935–1971,* vol. 1, *1935–1948* (New York: Ran-

dom House, 1972), 503–4, 512, 558.

3. McCullough, *Truman,* 383.

4. Robert J. Donovan, *Conflict and Crisis: The Presidency of Harry S. Truman, 1945–1948* (New York: W. W. Norton, 1977), 57.

5. McCullough, *Truman,* 451.

6. *Public Papers of the Presidents of the United States: Harry S. Truman, 1945* (Washington, D.C.: Government Printing Office, 1961), 209.

7. McCullough, *Truman,* 391.

8. Hamby, *Man of the People,* 331–32.

9. H. Truman, *Memoirs,* vol. 1, 416.

10. David Eisenhower, *Eisenhower at War, 1943–1945* (New York: Vintage Books, 1987), 692.

11. McCullough, *Truman,* 443; Hamby, *Man of the People,* 332.

12. McCullough, *Truman,* 413; M. Truman, *Where the Buck Stops,* 205–6.

13. M. Truman, *Where the Buck Stops,* 205.

14. Ibid., 204.

15. Winston S. Churchill, *The Second World War: Triumph and Tragedy* (New York: Bantam Books, 1962), 546.

16. Charles Bohlen, *Witness to History, 1929–1969* (New York: W. W. Norton, 1973), 231.

17. Hamby, *Man of the People,* 339.

18. John L. Gaddis, *The Long Peace: Inquiries into the History of the Cold War* (New York: Oxford University Press, 1987), 31–32.

19. H. Truman, *Memoirs,* vol. 1, 551–52.

20. Dallek, *Roosevelt and American Foreign Policy,* 517–19.

21. Donovan, *Conflict and Crisis,* chap. 16.

22. Burns, *Roosevelt,* 422–26.

23. Alonzo Hamby, *Beyond the New Deal: Harry S. Truman and American Liberalism* (New York: Columbia University Press, 1973), 61–62.

24. Donovan, *Conflict and Crisis,* 107.

25. Gallup, *Gallup Poll,* vol. 1, 558. Also, Donovan, *Conflict and Crisis,* 117.

26. Gallup, *Gallup Poll,* vol. 1, 528, 558.

27. Donovan, *Conflict and Crisis,* chap. 13; Hamby, *Beyond the New Deal,* chap. 3.

28. Donovan, *Conflict and Crisis,* 123, 125.

29. Robert Dallek, *Hail to the Chief: The Making and Unmaking of American Presidents* (New York: Hyperion, 1996), xii–xiii.

30. Robert Ferrell, ed., *Dear Bess: The Letters from Harry to Bess Truman, 1910–1959* (New York: W. W. Norton, 1983), 523–24.

3: THE WORST OF TIMES

1. T. D. Schellhardt, "Do We Expect Too Much?" *Wall Street Journal,* July 10, 1979.
2. McCullough, *Truman,* 481.
3. Ibid., 477.
4. Gallup, *Gallup Poll,* vol. 1, 499–500, 523, 558, 611.
5. Donovan, *Conflict and Crisis,* chap. 19.
6. McCullough, *Truman,* 493.
7. Ibid., 482.
8. H. Truman, *Memoirs,* vol. 1, 506.
9. Donovan, *Conflict and Crisis,* 127.
10. Gallup, *Gallup Poll,* vol. 1, 544–45, 566; Donovan, *Conflict and Crisis,* 128.
11. H. Truman, *Memoirs,* vol. 1, 509; *Public Papers of the Presidents: Harry S. Truman, 1946,* 15–16.
12. Donovan, *Conflict and Crisis,* 165; *Public Papers of the Presidents: Harry S. Truman, 1946,* 47–48.
13. Harry S. Truman, *Memoirs of Harry S. Truman,* vol. 2, *Years of Trial and Hope* (New York: Doubleday, 1956), 53–55.
14. Donovan, *Conflict and Crisis,* 198.
15. *Public Papers of the Presidents: Harry S. Truman, 1946,* 1ff.
16. Donovan, *Conflict and Crisis,* 164.
17. McCullough, *Truman,* 481–82, 492–506.

18. Hamby, *Beyond the New Deal*, 77.

19. Donovan, *Conflict and Crisis*, 121–22, 167, 198–99, 235–36.

20. Hamby, *Beyond the New Deal*, 78.

21. McCullough, *Truman*, 482, 485, 492–93.

22. Hamby, *Beyond the New Deal*, 83; McCullough, *Truman*, 485; Donovan, *Conflict and Crisis*, 236.

23. M. Truman, *Where the Buck Stops*, 81–82, 87.

24. Donovan, *Conflict and Crisis*, 170–71, 187; McCullough, *Truman*, 486.

25. Donovan, *Conflict and Crisis*, 187.

26. John L. Gaddis, *The United States and the Origins of the Cold War, 1941–1947* (New York: Columbia University Press, 1972), 302–4.

27. Ibid., 306–9, 312–15.

28. McCullough, *Truman*, 486–90.

29. Gaddis, *Origins of the Cold War*, 308–9, 314–15.

30. McCullough, *Truman*, 490.

31. Gaddis, *Origins of the Cold War*, 309–312; Hamby, *Man of the People*, 348–50.

32. Gaddis, *Origins of the Cold War*, 332–35; Donovan, *Conflict and Crisis*, 203–7; Hamby, *Man of the People*, 350–52; *Time*, September 30, 1946.

33. H. Truman, *Memoirs*, vol. 1, 555–60;

Donovan, *Conflict and Crisis,* 219–28; Mc-
Cullough, *Truman,* 513–18; Hamby, *Man
of the People,* 352–59.

34. Donovan, *Conflict and Crisis,* 229–38;
McCullough, *Truman,* 520–24.

35. Ralph Keyes, *The Wit and Wisdom of
Harry Truman* (New York: Gramercy Press,
1995), 57–60; Donovan, *Conflict and Crisis,* 239.

4: POLITICIAN AND STATESMAN

1. McCullough, *Truman,* 529.
2. Donovan, *Conflict and Crisis,* 245.
3. Ibid., 240.
4. Dallek, *Franklin D. Roosevelt and American Foreign Policy,* 388.
5. Donovan, *Conflict and Crisis,* 240, 242.
6. Gallup, *Gallup Poll,* vol. 1, 581, 606, 608,
610.
7. Donovan, *Conflict and Crisis,* 240–42;
Hamby, *Man of the People,* 419–20.
8. Gallup, *Gallup Poll,* vol. 1, 617, 623.
9. Donovan, *Conflict and Crisis,* 242–43.
10. For an excellent portrait of the Eightieth
Congress, see Donovan, *Conflict and Crisis,*
chap. 27, including the Wherry quote on
p. 258.
11. McCullough, *Truman,* 550–53.
12. Margaret Truman, *Harry S. Truman*

(New York: Pocket Books, 1973), 381–83; Donovan, *Conflict and Crisis,* chap. 32; Hamby, *Beyond the New Deal,* 184–85.

13. Donovan, *Conflict and Crisis,* 279–85.

14. Gallup, *Gallup Poll,* vol. 1, 636–37, 639; Ronald Steel, *Walter Lippmann and the American Century* (New York: Little, Brown, 1980), 438–39.

15. Gaddis, *Origins of the Cold War,* 348–52; Melvyn Leffler, *A Preponderance of Power: National Security, the Truman Administration, and the Cold War* (Palo Alto, Calif.: Stanford University Press, 1992), 121–27, 142–47.

16. McCullough, *Truman,* 561–65; H. Truman, *Memoirs,* vol. 2, 110–19; George F. Kennan, *Memoirs, 1925–1950* (New York: Little, Brown, 1967), chap. 14; Leffler, *Preponderance of Power,* 157–65; Arnold Offner, *Another Such Victory: President Truman and the Cold War, 1945–1953* (Palo Alto, Calif.: Stanford University Press, 2002), chap. 9.

17. The best recent analysis of the Marshall Plan is in Greg Behrman, *The Most Noble Adventure: The Marshall Plan and the Time When America Helped Save Europe* (New York: Free Press, 2007). Also see Niall Ferguson, "Dollar Diplomacy: How Much

Did the Marshall Plan Really Matter?" *The New Yorker,* August 27, 2007.

18. Michael J. Hogan, *A Cross of Iron: Harry S. Truman and the Origins of the National Security State, 1945–1954* (New York: Cambridge University Press, 1998), 24–68, 194–206.

19. McCullough, *Truman,* 483.

20. Ibid., 579–80.

21. Merle Miller, *Plain Speaking: An Oral Biography of Harry S. Truman* (New York: Berkeley Publishing, 1974), 230–32.

22. *Public Papers of the Presidents: Harry S. Truman, 1946,* 228; Donovan, *Conflict and Crisis,* 314, 315, 318–19.

23. John Morton Blum, *The Price of Vision: The Diary of Henry A. Wallace, 1942–1946* (Boston: Houghton Mifflin, 1973), 606–7.

24. *Public Papers of the Presidents: Harry S. Truman, 1946,* 442–44.

25. Donovan, *Conflict and Crisis,* 324–31. There is a well-drawn summary of Truman's views and actions leading up to the UN partition vote in Offner, *Another Such Victory,* 274–90.

26. Donovan, 243–45, 332–37; Hamby, *Beyond the New Deal,* 61–65, 188–90; McCullough, *Truman,* 569–70.

5: AGAINST ALL ODDS

1. McCullough, *Truman,* 584–86.
2. Ibid.
3. Gallup, *The Gallup Poll,* vol. 1, 623, 633, 636, 650, 665, 680.
4. Clark Clifford, *Counsel to the President* (New York: Random House, 1991), 189–94.
5. Ibid.
6. John C. Culver and John Hyde, *American Dreamer: A Life of Henry A. Wallace* (New York: W. W. Norton, 2000), 456–58.
7. Clifford, *Counsel to the President,* 194–96; McCullough, *Truman,* 585–86.
8. Clifford, *Counsel to the President,* 203–8; McCullough, *Truman,* 586–90.
9. Clifford, *Counsel to the President,* 208–209.
10. McCullough, *Truman,* 589; Hamby, *Beyond the New Deal,* 214–15.
11. Offner, *Another Such Victory,* 236–37; Leffler, *Preponderance of Power,* 204–9.
12. Offner, *Another Such Victory,* 238–40; Hogan, *Cross of Iron,* 145–46.
13. Donovan, *Conflict and Crisis,* 363–66.
14. Ibid., 367–68, 408–9, 423, 426, 436. Also see, Offner, *Another Such Victory,* chap. 10.
15. Gallup, *Gallup Poll,* vol. 1, 686–87; Lef-

fler, *Preponderance of Power,* 237–46.
16. Gallup, *Gallup Poll,* vol. 1, 722, 724–25, 727, 732, 734, 739, 745.
17. Hamby, *Man of the People,* 439.
18. Ibid., 441–44.
19. *Time,* June 28, 1948.
20. Gallup, *Gallup Poll,* vol. 1, 749.
21. McCullough, *Truman,* 612, 632–36.
22. Donovan, *Conflict and Crisis,* 388–89.
23. McCullough, *Truman,* 636–46.
24. Donovan, *Conflict and Crisis,* 410–12.
25. Gallup, *Gallup Poll,* vol. 1, 744–45, 747–48.
26. Ibid., 750–51, 753–54, 757, 759.
27. McCullough, *Truman,* chap. 14, especially 664, 670–72.

6: COLD WAR PRESIDENT

1. *Public Papers of the Presidents: Harry S Truman, 1948,* 941.
2. Hamby, *Beyond the New Deal,* chaps. 13 and 14.
3. Gallup, *Gallup Poll,* vol. 2, 780–83, 797, 801–5.
4. Hamby, *Beyond the New Deal,* 311–14.
5. Robert J. Donovan, *Tumultuous Years: The Presidency of Harry S. Truman, 1949–1953* (New York: W. W. Norton, 1982), 120–22.

6. Gallup, *Gallup Poll,* vol. 2, 787, 791, 808, 853.

7. Miller, *Plain Speaking,* 139.

8. Donovan, *Tumultuous Years,* chap. 3.

9. Leffler, *Preponderance of Power,* 208–18, 234–35, 280–86; Kennan, *Memoirs,* 407–11.

10. Leffler, *Preponderance of Power,* 9, 116, 313, 325–26; David E. Lilienthal, *The Journals of David Lilienthal, 1945–1950* (New York: Harper & Row, 1964), vol. 2, 570–71.

11. Gallup, *Gallup Poll,* vol. 2, 800, 815, 829–30, 834, 860, 867, 869.

12. Leffler, *Preponderance of Power,* 326–30; McCullough, *Truman,* 749, 756–58.

13. Offner, *Another Such Victory,* 347–57.

14. Quoted in Dallek, *Franklin D. Roosevelt and American Foreign Policy,* 328–29.

15. Offner, *Another Such Victory,* 329–37.

16. *The China White Paper, August 1949,* vol. 1 (Palo Alto, Calif.: Stanford University Press, 1967), iii–xvii; James Chace, *Acheson: The Secretary of State Who Created the American World* (New York: Simon & Schuster, 1998), 219–20.

17. Gallup, *Gallup Poll,* vol. 2, 852–53, 868–89.

18. Donovan, *Tumultuous Years,* 114–18.

1. *Public Papers of the Presidents: Harry S. Truman, 1950,* 2ff.; *New York Times,* January 5, 1950.

2. McCullough, *Truman,* 759–61.

3. Hamby, *Man of the People,* 529.

4. Leffler, *Preponderance of Power,* 327–33; McCullough, *Truman,* 761–64.

5. Offner, *Another Such Victory,* 365–67.

6. Dean Acheson, *Present at the Creation: My Years in the State Department* (New York: W. W. Norton, 1969), 374.

7. Gallup, *Gallup Poll,* vol. 2, 906–7.

8. Donovan, *Tumultuous Years,* chap. 16.

9. Ibid., 166, 168.

10. Leffler, *A Preponderance of Power,* 92–94.

11. Don Oberdorfer, *The Two Koreas: A Contemporary History* (Reading, Mass.: Addison-Wesley, 1997), 8–9.

12. Glenn D. Paige, *The Korean Decision, June 24–June 30, 1950* (New York: Free Press, 1968), part 3; Burton Kaufmann, *The Korean War* (Philadelphia: Temple University Press, 1986), chap. 1; Hamby, *Man of the People,* 534–39.

13. Leffler, *Preponderance of Power,* 364–69.

14. Ibid., 374–78.

15. Gallup, *Gallup Poll,* vol. 2, 943.

16. Hamby, *Man of the People,* 542–46.

17. Miller, *Plain Speaking,* 308, 315–17.

18. McCullough, *Truman,* 808–13.

19. Ibid., 813–14; the McCarthy quote is on p. 813.

20. Hamby, *Man of the People,* 549–51; the Schlesinger quote is on p. 551.

21. *Public Papers of the President: Harry S. Truman, 1950,* 714.

22. Leffler, *Preponderance of Power,* 398–400; Hamby, *Man of the People,* 551–52.

23. Leffler, *Preponderance of Power,* 400–401; Hamby, *Man of the People,* 552–53.

24. McCullough, *Truman,* 826–29; Miller, *Plain Speaking,* 87.

25. McCullough, *Truman,* 830.

26. Leffler, *Preponderance of Power,* 401–3; Hamby, *Man of the People,* 553.

8: Lost Credibility

1. Gallup, *Gallup Poll,* vol. 2, 958, 960–61, 964–65, 968–69, 972–73, 976–77.

2. John W. Spanier, *The Truman-MacArthur Controversy and the Korean War* (New York: W. W. Norton, 1965), chap. 10, especially 197–202.

3. Ibid., 202–7; Hamby, *Man of the People,* 555–56.

4. H. Truman, *Memoirs,* vol. 2, 436–50.

5. Miller, *Plain Speaking,* 308, 312–13.

6. H. Truman, *Memoirs,* vol. 2, 443–44; Spanier, *Truman-MacArthur Controversy,* 205–7.

7. Gallup, *Gallup Poll,* vol. 2, 981–82, 984, 987, 998.

8. Hamby, *Man of the People,* 561–64.

9. Spanier, *Truman-MacArthur Controversy,* 215–16, 219–20; Hamby, *Man of the People,* 561–62.

10. Michael Schaller, *Douglas MacArthur: The Far Eastern General* (New York: Oxford University Press, 1989), 242–43; William Manchester, *American Caesar: Douglas MacArthur, 1880–1964* (New York: Little, Brown, 1978), 612, 662; Gallup, *Gallup Poll,* vol. 2, 982, 998.

11. Manchester, *American Caesar,* 644.

12. Hamby, *Man of the People,* 558; Manchester, *American Caesar,* 644, 648–49.

13. Gallup, *Gallup Poll,* vol. 2, 989, 995, 999–1000.

14. H. Truman, *Memoirs,* vol. 2, 451–52; Hamby, *Man of the People,* 557–58, 562; Robert H. Ferrell, ed., *Off the Record* (New York: Harper & Row, 1980), 310.

15. H. Truman, *Memoirs,* vol. 2, 451; McCullough, *Truman,* 852–54.

16. McCullough, *Truman,* 853; Murray Polner, "Review of David Halberstam's *The Coldest Winter: America and the Korean War,*" on History News Network, November 12, 2007.

17. Offner, *Another Such Victory,* 406–9; Gallup, *Gallup Poll,* vol. 2, 1019, 1027.

18. Hamby, *Man of the People,* 574.

19. Gallup, *Gallup Poll,* vol. 2, 1007, 1019–22, 1032.

20. David Oshinsky, *A Conspiracy So Immense: The World of Joe McCarthy* (New York: Free Press, 1983), chaps. 12–15; McCullough, *Truman,* 860–62; Robert Dallek, *Lone Star Rising: Lyndon Johnson and His Times, 1908–1960* (New York: Oxford University Press, 1991), 451–59; *New York Review of Books,* November 22, 2007, p. 25.

21. Gallup, *Gallup Poll,* vol. 2, 1007–8; Leffler, *Preponderance of Power,* 391–93.

22. Leffler, *Preponderance of Power,* 408–13.

23. Gallup, *Gallup Poll,* vol. 2, 1010, 1016–18; Hamby, *Man of the People,* 575–80.

24. McCullough, *Truman,* 862–72.

9: LAST HURRAHS

1. Gallup, *Gallup Poll,* vol. 2, 977–78, 997, 1015, 1021–22, 1038.
2. Donovan, *Tumultuous Years,* 171–72, 392.
3. Ibid., chap. 35; Hamby, *Man of the People,* 589–93.
4. Donovan, *Tumultuous Years,* chap. 36; McCullough, *Truman,* 895–903; Hamby, *Man of the People,* 593–98.
5. Offner, *Another Such Victory,* 409–17.
6. Donovan, *Tumultuous Years,* 392–401; Hamby, *Man of the People,* 599–614; McCullough, *Truman,* 887–913.
7. Donovan, *Tumultuous Years,* 402–404; McCullough, *Truman,* 920–21; Hamby, *Man of the People,* 614–18.
8. McCullough, *Truman,* 918–20.
9. Hamby, *Man of the People,* 618.

EPILOGUE

1. The material in the epilogue is drawn from McCullough, *Truman,* chap. 18; and Hamby, *Man of the People,* chap. 34.
2. Robert Dallek, *An Unfinished Life: John F. Kennedy, 1917–1963* (New York: Little, Brown, 2003), 235.
3. McCullough, *Truman,* 966.
4. Ibid., 978.
5. Hamby, *Man of the People,* 632.

MILESTONES

1884

Born on May 8 in Lamar, Missouri, a farm community 120 miles south of Kansas City.

1890

The Truman family moves to Independence, Missouri, a rural town, ten miles southeast of Kansas City.

1901

Harry graduates from high school. He gives up thoughts of attending college to help support his family.

1906

After working for five years in a succession of jobs in Kansas City, he leaves a well-paying bank clerkship to work on the family farm.

1917

Truman becomes a captain of artillery in a National Guard unit. He distinguishes himself in combat.

1919

In June, after discharge from the army, he marries Elizabeth (Bess) Wallace, his childhood sweetheart.

1922

A haberdashery store he and Eddie Jacobson, an army buddy, had opened in downtown Kansas City fails in a recession. Truman launches a political career with the support of Kansas City's Pendergast machine, winning election as eastern district judge of Jackson County.

1926

He wins election as the county's presiding judge.

1934

He wins election to the United States Senate.

1940

He wins reelection to the Senate and establishes a national reputation by chairing a subcommittee that investigates war profiteering and industrial waste.

1944

Truman is chosen as Franklin Roosevelt's running mate and is elected vice president.

1945

Franklin Roosevelt's death on April 12 elevates Truman to the presidency. Germany's surrender in May ends World War II in Europe. Truman meets with Churchill and Stalin in July at Potsdam to discuss the Pacific war and postwar arrangements. In August, he orders the use of atomic bombs against Hiroshima and Nagasaki, which forces Japan's surrender.

1946

George Kennan's "long telegram" warns against Soviet dangers. In March, in a speech in Missouri, Churchill describes an Iron Curtain dividing Europe. In September, after Henry Wallace publicly attacks the president's anti-Soviet policy, Truman fires him. In November, the Republicans recapture both houses of Congress.

1947

In response to mounting pressures about subversion by domestic Communists, Truman sets up a Federal Employees Loyalty and Security Program. In March, Truman announces the Truman Doctrine to help Greece and Turkey fight Communist subversion. In June, Secretary of State George Marshall proposes a $16.5 billion European reconstruction plan. The Republican Congress passes the anti–labor union Taft-Hartley bill over Truman's veto. In October, a Truman-appointed committee issues a civil rights report urging equal rights for African Americans. Truman declares his support for a Jewish homeland in Palestine.

1948

As part of an election strategy, Truman announces plans for a Fair Deal that includes a civil rights bill enforcing equal rights for blacks. A Communist coup in Czechoslovakia and a West European Union to meet the Communist threat intensifies the cold war. A Communist blockade of West Berlin in response to the reestablishment of a German state moves Truman to initiate a Berlin airlift. Truman recognizes the new state of Israel. In the fall, Truman runs a brilliant and victorious election campaign that upsets predictions that Governor Thomas Dewey of New York would take back the White House for the Republicans. A preoccupation with Communist dangers at home (the Alger Hiss case) and abroad (Soviet detonation of an atomic bomb and a Communist victory over the Nationalists in China) make it impossible for Truman to win significant domestic reforms promised in his Fair Deal. Truman responds to Communist advances by agreeing to U.S. leadership of the North Atlantic Treaty Organization (NATO). The publication of

The White Paper asserts U.S. inability to shape events in China.

1950

Truman instructs defense officials to proceed with plans to develop hydrogen bombs. NSC-68 outlines a military buildup and strategy for defeating worldwide communism. Senator Joseph McCarthy airs public accusations of Communist subversion by State Department officials. In June, North Korea attacks South Korea. Truman decides to use U.S. forces to defeat the aggression. General Douglas MacArthur beats back North Korea's attack through an amphibious landing at Inchon. After a meeting with MacArthur on Wake Island, Truman gives MacArthur permission to cross the 38th parallel to destroy the Communist regime. In November, the Chinese respond to the U.S.–South Korean advance to the Yalu River with an invasion of North Korea that drives U.S. forces back below the 38th parallel. In congressional elections, frustrations over Korea, the cold war, and inflation narrow the Democratic Party's control of both houses of Congress.

1951

The fighting in Korea becomes a stalemate. MacArthur's public demands for a more aggressive strategy lead Truman to dismiss him. Accusations of administration corruption drive Truman's approval ratings down to a new low of 23 percent.

1952

Truman attempts to seize the steel mills to head off a strike, which the Supreme Court rules unconstitutional. With his public approval at low levels, Truman announces that he will not run for another term. The Republicans nominate Dwight Eisenhower and the Democrats nominate Adlai Stevenson for the presidency. The Republicans win a decisive victory, taking the White House and both houses of Congress.

1953

Truman returns to Independence.

1955

Publication of the first volume of his memoirs.

1957

Opening of the Truman Library.

1960

Truman takes an active role in the presidential campaign, first opposing John F. Kennedy and then supporting him in the general election against Richard Nixon.

1965

Lyndon Johnson signs Medicare bill in

Independence as a tribute to Truman.

1972

Dies on December 26, at the age of eighty-eight.

SELECTED BIBLIOGRAPHY

Acheson, Dean. *Present at the Creation: My Years in the State Department.* New York: W. W. Norton, 1969.

Barkley, Alben. *That Reminds Me — The Autobiography of the Veep.* Garden City, N.Y.: Doubleday, 1954.

Behrman, Greg. *The Most Noble Adventure: The Marshall Plan and the Time When America Helped Save Europe.* New York: Free Press, 2007.

Blum, John Morton. *The Price of Vision: The Diary of Henry A. Wallace, 1942–1946.* Boston: Houghton Mifflin, 1973.

Bohlen, Charles. *Witness to History, 1929–1969.* New York: W. W. Norton, 1973.

Burns, James MacGregor. *Roosevelt: The Soldier of Freedom.* New York: Harcourt Brace Jovanovich, 1970.

Chace, James. *Acheson: The Secretary of State Who Created the American World.*

New York: Simon & Schuster, 1998.

The China White Paper, August 1949. 2 vols. Palo Alto, Calif.: Stanford University Press, 1967.

Churchill, Winston S. *The Second World War: Triumph and Tragedy.* New York: Bantam Books, 1962.

Clifford, Clark. *Counsel to the President.* New York: Random House, 1991.

Culver, John C., and John Hyde. *American Dreamer: A Life of Henry A. Wallace.* New York: W. W. Norton, 2000.

Dallek, Robert. *Franklin D. Roosevelt and American Foreign Policy, 1932–1945.* New York: Oxford University Press, 1995.

———. *Hail to the Chief: The Making and Unmaking of American Presidents.* New York: Hyperion, 1996.

———. *Lone Star Rising: Lyndon Johnson and His Times, 1908–1960.* New York: Oxford University Press, 1991.

———. *An Unfinished Life: John F. Kennedy, 1917–1963.* New York: Little, Brown, 2003.

Donovan, Robert J. *Conflict and Crisis: The Presidency of Harry S. Truman, 1945–1948.* New York: W. W. Norton, 1977.

———. *Tumultuous Years: The Presidency of Harry S. Truman, 1949–1953.* New York:

W. W. Norton, 1982.

Eisenhower, David. *Eisenhower at War, 1943–1945.* New York: Vintage Books, 1987.

Ferrell, Robert (ed.). *Dear Bess: The Letters from Harry to Bess Truman, 1910–1959.* New York: W. W. Norton, 1983.

———. *Off the Record: The Private Papers of Harry S. Truman.* New York: Harper & Row, 1980.

Gaddis, John L. *The Long Peace: Inquiries into the History of the Cold War.* New York: Oxford University Press, 1987.

———. *The United States and the Origins of the Cold War, 1941–1947.* New York: Columbia University Press, 1972.

Gallup, George H. *The Gallup Poll, 1935–1971.* 3 vols. Vol. 1: *1935–1948;* Vol. 2: *1949–1958.* New York: Random House, 1972.

Halberstam, David. *The Coldest Winter: America and the Korean War.* New York: Hyperion, 2007.

Hamby, Alonzo L. *Beyond the New Deal: Harry S. Truman and American Liberalism.* New York: Columbia University Press, 1973.

———. *Man of the People: A Life of Harry S. Truman.* New York: Oxford University

Press, 1995.

Hogan, Michael J. *A Cross of Iron: Harry S. Truman and the Origins of the National Security State, 1945–1954.* New York: Cambridge University Press, 1998.

Kaufmann, Burton. *The Korean War.* Philadelphia: Temple University Press, 1986.

Kennan, George F. *Memoirs, 1925–1950.* New York: Little, Brown, 1967.

Keyes, Ralph. *The Wit and Wisdom of Harry Truman.* New York: Gramercy Press, 1995.

Leffler, Melvyn. *A Preponderance of Power: National Security, the Truman Administration, and the Cold War.* Palo Alto, Calif.: Stanford University Press, 1992.

Lilienthal, David E. *The Journals of David Lilienthal, 1945–1950.* 2 vols. New York: Harper & Row, 1964.

Manchester, William. *American Caesar: Douglas MacArthur, 1880–1964.* New York: Little, Brown, 1978.

McCullough, David. *Truman.* New York: Simon & Schuster, 1992.

Miller, Merle. *Plain Speaking: An Oral Biography of Harry S. Truman.* New York: Berkeley Publishing, 1974.

Oberdorfer, Don. *The Two Koreas: A Contemporary History.* Reading, Mass.: Addison-Wesley, 1997.

Offner, Arnold. *Another Such Victory: President Truman and the Cold War, 1945–1953.* Stanford, Calif.: Stanford University Press, 2002.

Oshinsky, David. *A Conspiracy So Immense: The World of Joe McCarthy.* New York: Free Press, 1983.

Paige, Glenn D. *The Korean Decision, June 24–June 30, 1950.* New York: Free Press, 1968.

Public Papers of the Presidents of the United States: Harry S. Truman, 1945–1952. 8 vols. Washington, D.C.: Government Printing Office, 1961.

Rovere, Richard, and Arthur Schlesinger Jr. *General MacArthur and President Truman: The Struggle for Control of American Foreign Policy.* New Brunswick, N.J.: Transactions, 1992.

Schaller, Michael. *Douglas MacArthur: The Far Eastern General.* New York: Oxford University Press, 1989.

Schlesinger, Arthur M., Jr. *The Cycles of American History.* Boston: Houghton Mifflin, 1989.

Spanier, John W. *The Truman-MacArthur Controversy and the Korean War.* New York: W. W. Norton, 1965.

Steel, Ronald. *Walter Lippmann and the*

American Century. New York: Little, Brown, 1980.

Truman, Harry S. *The Autobiography of Harry S. Truman.* Columbia: University of Missouri Press, 2002.

————. *Memoirs of Harry S. Truman.* Vol. 1: *Year of Decisions.* New York: Doubleday, 1955.

————. *Memoirs of Harry S. Truman.* Vol 2: *Years of Trial and Hope.* New York: Doubleday, 1956.

Truman, Margaret. *Harry S. Truman.* New York: Pocket Books, 1974.

———— (ed.). *Where the Buck Stops: The Personal and Private Writings of Harry S. Truman.* New York: Warner Books, 1989.

Wolfe, Thomas. *You Can't Go Home Again.* New York: Harper and Brothers, 1940.

ABOUT THE AUTHOR

Robert Dallek is the author of several bestselling presidential histories, including *Nixon and Kissinger: Partners in Power; An Unfinished Life: John F. Kennedy, 1917–1963;* and the classic two-volume biography of Lyndon Johnson *Lone Star Rising* and *Flawed Giant.* He has taught at Columbia, Oxford, UCLA, Boston University, Dartmouth, and Stanford in Washington, and has won the Bancroft Prize, among numerous other awards for scholarship and teaching. He lives in Washington, D.C.

The employees of Thorndike Press hope you have enjoyed this Large Print book. All our Thorndike and Wheeler Large Print titles are designed for easy reading, and all our books are made to last. Other Thorndike Press Large Print books are available at your library, through selected bookstores, or directly from us.

For information about titles, please call:
(800) 223-1244

or visit our Web site at:
http://gale.cengage.com/thorndike

To share your comments, please write:
Publisher
Thorndike Press
295 Kennedy Memorial Drive
Waterville, ME 04901